LESBIAN LOVE

WOMEN IN LOVE THROUGHOUT THE AGES

WALTER BRAUN

Translation and additional material by
Rudolf Schlesinger

SENATE

Lesbian Love

First published in 1966 by Luxor Press Ltd, London.

This edition published in 1996 by Senate,
an imprint of Random House UK Ltd,
Random House, 20 Vauxhall Bridge Road,
London SW1V 2SA.

ISBN 1 85170 556 2

Printed and bound in Great Britain by
Cox & Wyman, Reading, Berkshire

CONTENTS

INTRODUCTION

Why this Book was Written

Up till some years ago I had only a very superficial idea of the difficulties and problems lesbians have to face. My knowledge of lesbianism was limited to some facts and theories any psychiatrist knows and most of this information was to be found in almost any textbook on homosexuality.

Then something happened that changed my entire attitude to lesbianism.

One day, in the course of a consultation, I asked a woman patient to write down for me, at some length, the whole background of her problems. She wrote to me about her homosexuality and gave me all the details about her life, her fears and longings, about her love towards other women and the way she made love to them.

It was a startling *document humain* and it convinced me of the fact that there was more in lesbianism than we teach our students in medical school. This confession—the reader will find it reproduced complete in this study of lesbianism —made me see female homosexuality in a new and different light. Suddenly I knew the task I had to set myself. I had to write a book on lesbians. This time however it would not be a book that rehashed all the old—and often outdated—facts. My book was going to be different. For the first time a detailed history of lesbianism would be written. New case histories, never before published, were going to illustrate my theories. New information would shed a fresh light on sexual interests that are fashionable nowadays.

While doing research for my book I interviewed hundreds of lesbians. Most of them told me everything I wanted to know. They even discussed their ways of love making and of getting sexual satisfaction in intimate detail. I knew then my book was not going to be for the prude. In writing this study I had to call a spade a spade and no false sense of decency should stop me from giving vital information, even about the most intimate things of a woman's life, to the reader with a sincere interest in this subject.

I knew this was a dangerous decision. Mrs Grundy never sleeps, and too easily the men and women who think it their job to watch over the morals of our society are filled with indignation about "offences against morality" committed in literature and in serious textbooks. I knew however that it was a risk to be taken. Only if the whole truth and nothing but the truth is known and nothing is suppressed because it is "shameful", "indecent", or even "obscene", can a society grow up.

This book is the consequence of the confession a lesbian patient wrote to me. A shameless confession? Yes, the reader can see that for himself. But an indecent or even obscene one? No, I don't think so. For every intimate detail mentioned in that story and enlarged upon in this book, concerns human actions, arising from human emotions, born out of the love of one human being for another.

CHAPTER ONE

Lesbianism in Antiquity

Though the book herewith offered to the public is mainly an attempt to describe the position of lesbian love-life today, from a psychiatrist's point of view, we nevertheless believe that a historical survey of this curious phenomenon cannot be omitted. Not only because today is unthinkable and inexplicable without yesterday, but because in the literature devoted to lesbian love the historical element is not only generally neglected, but at the same time often misinterpreted. One can safely say that the French doctor Martineau[1] was quite right when he stated in 1905, "This question [of lesbianism] is rather unknown, and nevertheless one of the most exciting problems for the doctor and the historian." Still this doctor must have possessed a very scanty knowledge of history, for not only is sexual intercourse between women itself as old as history, but the facts known about it date back to the most remote times too.

Already in the Talmud lesbian love is mentioned and the term always used in this respect, *solédeth*, i.e. "to jump, hop and frisk the one on the other", leaves no doubt about the sexual character of these relationships. One even finds in the Talmud an outspoken tendency to treat lesbian women exactly in the same way as prostitutes *from the point of law*. Still the general feeling about sexual intercourse between women did nothing else than cause a sort of moral indignation, which was not strong enough to make it necessary to establish laws against it. This same

11

attitude we find in the New Testament, for though Ploss and Bartels[2] are of opinion that the Bible does not name the phenomenon, the Apostle Paul certainly means lesbian love, when, in his Epistle to the Romans, he speaks of women who "did change the natural use into that which is against nature" and in the same letter states "and likewise also the men, leaving the natural use of the women, burned in their lust one toward another; men with men working that which is unseemly." We think it even logical that the Apostle Paul thought it necessary to warn against lesbian love, as about the time that Christianity originated, the Roman Empire was in absolute decay and amidst the general immorality that such a situation caused, lesbian love flourished in such a special way that the term *amor lesbicus* became common in Latin literature (see Martial, Juvenal, Tertullian, Petronius and others). Apart from all literary references about lesbian love, we even possess a most bizarre literal proof of the phenomenon.

During the excavations of Pompeii, entirely destroyed by volcanic eruptions in 78 A.D., two apparently female skeletons were found; these skeletons were twisted in such an attitude—the hand of one woman resting on the mount of Venus of the other—that the lesbian character of this find was beyond all doubt.[3]

Though on the surface a circumstance of minor importance only, we still would like to stress the point that the house in which the skeletons were discovered had obviously been a lupanar or *brothel*, because exactly the brothel has played an important role in sexual life between women during all ages. Always the connection between lesbianism and prostitution has been close, and there is no essential difference between the Roman matrons visiting their prostitute-friends—a fact mentioned, for instance, by Lucian— and the better-class German women after the First World War trying to establish lesbian contacts in such notorious "night-clubs" as "Dorian Gray", "Olala", etc. Numerous examples of these sexual relationships between the inmates

12

of the brothel and their female customers we find cited in classics like Rosenbaum's *Geschichte der Lustseuche* (1839) in Parent-Duchâtelet's *La Prostitution dans la ville de Paris* (1836), in Martineau's *La Prostitution clandestine à Paris* (1897), and apart from this the ample evidence of lesbian contacts of prostitutes among themselves has effected such an influence upon general thinking that the "sapphic prostitute" has even become a theme in literature and art. In this respect we have only to refer either to Zola's *Nana* or to the masterly drawings of Foujita, Grosz and von Bayros.

SAPPHO AND HER POETRY

As we have introduced in the last paragraph the term "sapphic" and as we have spoken continuously about "lesbian love" when dealing with sexual intercourse between women, we think it to be appropriate to explain these two words, especially as this explanation fits into the pattern of our historical survey.

Sappho was a brilliant poetess, who lived on the little isle of Lesbos in the Aegean Sea.* The first author who accused Sappho of having been a "woman-lover" was Lucian, who lived from 125–200 A.D., which means about 750 years after Sappho died. Though both the personality and the poetry of Sappho had been dealt with often already, no one before Lucian ever tried to make Sappho out as a woman-lover. It was a well-known fact that Lucian did not take truth very seriously when it did not fit into the pattern of his satirical poems, because of which he has become so famous (Lucian: *Dialogues of Courtesans* 5, 2: "I suppose you mean she is one of those women who don't care about men, but enjoy having women, as if they were men themselves, like the women of Lesbos?") Nevertheless Domitius Calderinus (about 1450) stated on the basis of Lucian's "information" that Sappho had been a

* The island is nowadays known as Mytilene,

13

lover of women, and from that moment on sexual intercourse between women was called either "lesbianism" or "sapphism". Joh. Britannicus, a professor who lived in Brescia about 1480, did not even mention any eventualities or arguments but flatly stated that Sappho had been a "tribade", i.e. a woman-lover, and from these decades on the myth about the poetess definitely had been born. It had a long life, and only in the beginning of the nineteenth century some contradiction arose, though even then an authority like Virey believed in the old ideas about Sappho. But men like Moncaut, Henne am Rhyn and J. J. Bachofen[4] tried to rebuild the personality of Sappho by means of her poetry and of the mores of the epoch of which she had been a child. And gradually grew the conviction that this woman hardly could have been the "Lesbian Madonna" into which tradition had moulded her.

Now who was Sappho?

Sappho was born on Lesbos and lived from about 630–560 B.C. She came from a well-to-do family, probably lower "island-aristocracy". Though she had two brothers, the youngest, Charaxos, was the one she cared for. Now this young man fell in love with a prostitute called "Rhodopis" (i.e. the one with the rosy cheeks) on one of his trips to Egypt. Even when this unimportant affair had come to an end, Sappho could still not stop lecturing her brother about his misbehaviour. To some psychoanalysts this undoubtedly will prove that indeed Sappho had been a homosexual, since her attitude in this affair proved that she could not stand the idea of another woman being possessed by a man, i.e. her brother. To other psychoanalysts her behaviour will clearly show that Sappho was quite normal because her reactions proved how she had the welfare of her brother (a man) at heart. Whatever the truth might have been, the only certainty we have is, that because of the political intrigues of the time in which her father was involved, she had to move to Sicily, where, at the age of 20, she married a man called Kerkylas. Out of this marriage

14

two children were born. Even though this typical heterosexual fact seems not to convince Forberg in his *Apophoreta* of Sappho's love for men, we do presume that the following fragments of her poetry indicate clearly enough her natural tendencies. Fragment No. 99: "Happy man, your wants now have been fulfilled, you have reached your goal. . . ." Fragment No. 104: "With whom, with what, you young husband, can I compare you? I know you are like the sveltest tree. . . ."

Hardly a homosexual woman could have written poetry of this kind! What has maintained then—apart from Lucian's notorious verses—the myth of Sappho's homosexuality? The key to it we think can be found in Fragment No. 85: "A sweet child I have, a golden flower alike as far as its body is concerned. I would not give you away for the whole of Lydia, nor for the beautiful Lesbos I shall ever leave you, dear Klais . . .", because to the "routine-thinkers" it only proved how immensely she was in love with girls. But we think, with Bachofen, that though this fragment certainly contains the key to Sappho's morals, the contents of the key is to be explained quite differently. She was not in love with girls, she was in love with her girls (as Klais was her daughter), with children. Rightly Bachofen mentions in his book: "The efforts of Sappho were directed to the education of her own sex. What never seem to be united—love and sex—happen here in the kindest way." And when we have taken into consideration the life Sappho led when she had come back from Sicily, Bachofen's opinions become quite clear. Sappho, now older, and whose husband had died in the meantime, had created an institute, in a way to be compared with the institute of Mutter Henschel (which was built after the idea of the German poet Stefan George), the intention of which was to educate the girls of the better classes, according to the standards and morals of those days. And when one reads about her lectures on philosophy, poetry, dancing, singing, flower-arranging, etc., one wonders how 2500 years later

15

men like Paul Brandt in his *Sapho* and Steiner in his *Sapho* still can speak of the "lesbian" Sappho, though even apart from all this the well-known philologue Fr. Welcker[5] has proved so evidently the heterosexuality of this woman. In fact Sappho was a heterosexual, who in her attitude towards girls under her care can be compared with the attitude Socrates took to the boys he had to educate. As we nevertheless still shall use the terms "lesbian love" and "sapphic" we do this only because of traditional reasons, and because of the fact that words like "tribade" or "frictrice" or "urning", for women who have sexual intercourse with women, do not have any meaning to the general public any more.

LESBIANISM IN CLASSICAL AND EARLY CHRISTIAN TIMES

The term frictrice brings us back to the point where we left our historical survey, the situation in Rome during the beginning of Christianity. Not only was sexual intercourse between women so widespread that, as we said, the term *amor lesbicus* was common in literature, but the word the *vox populi* gave to this type of women, *frictrices* (i.e. "they who rub their clitoris") indicates even that the intimate technical aspects lesbian-love acts include, were no secret at all, but apparently well known to the general public. Here we strike at once at one of the most remarkable aspects of sex-life during the ancient times in general and during classical antiquity in particular, namely the fact that the terminology used both in ordinary language and in literature was of such a direct rudeness that it proves the straightforward approach man had in sex-matters. With the same ease as the Romans spoke about their *frictrices* the Greeks gossiped about their *tribades* i.e. "the ones that rub" their clitoris, and one is overwhelmed by the number of anecdotes about for example the ways the

16

clitoris could be enlarged so that intercourse between women could be more satisfactory. It can be safely stated that both in Rome and in Greece it was general knowledge that lesbians tried to enlarge their clitoris by (mutual) rubbing and by artificial means, to give it the look and effect of the masculine member. One wonders how and why this extreme attention to the clitoris has not earlier led to the conclusions Freud later drew when publishing his theory of "Penis-envy" and one certainly wonders about the slow motions of the human mind in this respect, when considering the "Olisbos", the leather artificial phallus, so often met with in Greek literature and art. (See Forberg in his *De Figuris Veneris* and Wilhelm Klein in his *Griechische Vasen mit Lieblingsinschriften*, Leipzig 1898—where we can admire a beautiful drawing on which a woman puts the artificial penis in her body with the left hand, while keeping in her right the little bottle of oil, necessary to ease the procedure.)

However important in practice this artificial phallus might have been, it still never has been able to play the role the clitoris obtained in the literature concerning lesbian love. The importance attached to the function of the clitoris in sexual intercourse between women went so far, that there existed a stern belief in the possibilities of cohabitation by means of the clitoris. Not even a scholar like Forberg could escape this conception (compare his chapter about the tribades in his *Apophoreta*), though we think, in accordance with Rohleder[6], that when a thing like this happened at all, it only could have been possible in the exceptional cases where the clitoris was enlarged in such an abnormal way, that immission of it into the body of the partner was possible. There exist some French doctors who claim to have known some of these cases, but still, as we have said already, these must have been remarkably uncommon. (This belief of cohabitation by means of the clitoris becomes quite normal, of course, when one is willing to accept statements like the one, for instance, of Nicolas

17

Plater, who flatly states having seen a lesbian woman with a clitoris as long as the neck of a goose. In the same tradition Venette[7] narrates that in the eleventh century an Egyptian doctor named Rodahamid had to castrate the wife of the sultan, as her clitoris had got such dimensions that sexual intercourse between her and her husband had become rather awkward.) Still further in his conclusions about the possibilities in lesbian love-life went a man like Duhousset, who claims to have witnessed a case where a sapphian had become pregnant by means of sexual intercourse with another tribade. As this case is a typical example of the superstitions still existing in some circles of the medical world at the end of the last century, we think it appropriate to cite it in detail, since it shows what wishful thinking can produce in the mind of a learned man.

Duhousset then tells us how two women (in Egypt) had a lesbian affair, which relationship was continued after the marriage of one of them. Now, according to our author, the one not married became pregnant, and enthusiastically Duhousset accepts this fact as waterproof evidence for the possibilities of pregnancy between lesbian women. It seems more probable that the married one after having had intercourse with her husband, kept the ejaculated semen inside, and gave some of it to her girl friend in the embrace following immediately after the sexual act with the husband.

Though most of what has been said up till now only shows that in Greece and Rome lesbian love did exist, it does not mean that the Middle East and Far East were free from the phenomenon. But as classical antiquity has been one of the principal pillars of our civilisation, we thought it logical to focus our attention on Greece and Rome first. With the second pillar of today's culture, Christianity, we shall be confronted next.

One could ask why Christianity had to react noticeably in respect of female homosexuality, since, first of all, homosexuality in general was a widespread acknowledged phenomenon, secondly the laws in classical antiquity reflected this attitude and tolerated it, unless it concerned circumstances where violence or abuse of power (directed against liberated slaves, for instance) were involved. The only case known to us where women were punished because of tribadism concerns the vestal virgins, and as these priestesses were punishable as well when they had had sexual intercourse with men, not the sexual act itself was condemnable, but the breach of their promise of eternal chastity, and so one can hardly speak in this particular case of a law against lesbian love directly.

Still, to our opinion, Christianity had to react, because according to the Biblical conception homosexuality was a typically pagan sin which had not only abased the standards of morality and weakened the physical strength of the people, but consequently had ruined empires as well. This despite the fact that the old reliable historians had amply shown how homosexuality, both female and male, was already widespread and acknowledged before Hellas and Rome had reached their zenith. So gradually the first laws against homosexuality were born; all the same, the edicts given by the Emperors Constantine the Great and Valentinianus during the fourth century A.D. sprang more from the consideration that homosexuality weakened the spirit and body of the people, than out of moral conviction or indignation. Though Constantine's edict contains neither exactly the character of the punishable offence (he only refers to the "coitus against nature"—in the sense of pedicatio, which means literally the *immissio in anum*—either done by men or women), nor the exact character of the punishment. Valentinianus' edict threatens the culprits, women and men, with being burned alive. In his commentaries on this law, Valentinianus states "we cannot tolerate that our sacred Rome, mother of all virtues, is any longer soiled by the sin of homosexuality"[8]. One wonders how a man like Augustinus, who lived during the same period, and who undoubtedly was a homosexual[9] must have felt when reading these empty, demogogical words. Nevertheless, the first legal measures against lesbian intercourse had been established, though we still have to realise that even the changed governmental outlook was not a definite death-blow to tribadism, as the new laws were mainly directed against a few homosexual variations—especially against "immission into the rectum", either done "naturally" by man, or "unnaturally" by woman—while the most prac-tised lesbian acts like mutual masturbation, the use of an artificial phallus (as long as not put *in anum*!), cunnilingus etc., could be safely performed, being not legally punish-able. We surely can consider the edicts of Constantine and Valentinianus as the basis upon which the whole law-making against homosexuality until very recently was built. Of course there existed local differences, but as civilisation during the period 400–1900 was mainly dominated by Christianity and Roman Law, the measures taken against male and female homosexuality show great uniformity.

As a striking example of both this similarity and con-tinuity in law-making, we want to cite the "Lex Romana Visigothorum" made during the reign of King Alarich II, which is not only based on the jurisdiction of Valentinianus, but mentions the same sexual acts as being punishable; even the kind of punishments for these derelictions do not differ from those of the Emperor's code. It certainly is tragic to see how the sound laws of the tribes of the Saxons and Franks gradually disappear under the rapidly growing in-fluence of the clergy; far more tragic, however, is the cir-cumstance that this same Lex Romana of the fifth century was in the twelfth century still used as the most authorita-tive law-reference, in all those countries where Roman Law and Christianity had been the decisive factors in the con-ception of moral and legal standards, such as Austria, Germany, Spain, France, Belgium, and Holland, among others.

We regret having included so many legal details in the foregoing, but as one could nearly say that the various legislation is our only source of proof of the existence of a lesbian love-life during the beginning of Christianity and the early Middle Ages, it simply was a necessity to recount these details because, though we can easily *guess* that "Das deutsche Badewesen" as described in all its extravagance by Rudeck[10] might have led to sapphism, and because though we are certain that the sexual perversions practised in nunneries under the mask of religious ecstasy must have included lesbian sex-acts, still the factual details are not profuse. In the next chapter, however, we shall deal with the matter in more detail.

NOTES

1. Martineau, *Deformations Vulvaires et Anales*, Paris 1905.

2. Ploss and Bartels, *Das Weib in der Natur- und Völkerkunde*, Leipzig 1 13.

3. Franz Scott, *Das Lesbische Weib*, Berlin c. 1930.

4. Moncaut, *Histoire de l'Amour dans l'Antiquité chez les Hébreux, les Orientaux, les Grecs et les Romains*, Paris 1862; Henne am Rhyn, *Die Frau i.d. Kulturgeschichte*, Berlin 1892; J. J. Bachofen, *Das Mutterrecht, eine Untersuchung über die Gynaikokratie der alten Welt nach ihrer religiösen und rechtlichen Natur*, Basel 1897.

5. Fr. Welcker, *Sapho von einem herrschenden Vorurteil befreit.*

6. Rohleder, *Vorlesungen über Geschlechtstrieb und gesamtes Geschechtsleben*, Vol. 2.

7. Nicolas Venette, *De la génération de l'homme ou Tableau de l'amour conjugal*, 1696.

8. See *Jahrbücher für sexuelle Zwischenstufen*, Vol. 1.

9. See *Jahrbücher für sexuelle Zwischenstufen*, Vol. 1.

10. W. Rudeck, *Geschichte der öffentlichen Sittlichkeit in Deutschland*, Jena 1897.

CHAPTER TWO

Centuries of Lesbianism and the Situation Today

Strange as it seems the pious Middle Ages brought a revival of lesbianism. The all-important part religion played during these centuries in western Europe could not prevent sexual excesses from being the order of the day. Religious-minded men and women flagellated each other to renounce the world and its vanities and found sexual gratification in their actions. The same could be said of saints who endured masochistic humiliations, just to be worthy to enter the Kingdom of Heaven—simple-minded people who did not dream of associating the inflicted punishments and humiliations with the sexual gratification they felt and could only try harder to keep their body and desires under control.

The naïvety of mediaeval monks and nuns was incredible. Female saints sang the praise of Christ's person and described how they should like to love the divine body—an attitude that will be recognised by any psychiatrist as an act of crypto-sexuality.

Of course it is unjust to judge mediaeval people—their customs, beliefs and actions—by modern standards. Nevertheless it is amazing that religious leaders in the Middle Ages did not see the backgrounds of many actions of their pupils. One of the best examples of a saint, who was just a complete masochist but was not recognised then as one, is St Mary Magdalene de Pazzi.

St Mary Magdalene de Pazzi lived in the sixteenth century in Italy. She was a member of one of the branches of the very famous Pazzi family of Florence. When twelve years old the only thing that interested her was religion. Two years earlier she had made a vow of virginity and perpetual chastity, "which", as her biographer Dingwall[1] remarks, "rather suggests that she must have been a remarkably precocious child and withal a somewhat unpleasant one."

When she was fourteen years old the girl entered the convent of San Giovannino in the city of Cortona in Tuscany. Sister Mary had already made it a custom then to administer herself very severe whippings which were meant to dispel worldly temptations. At the same time she experienced regularly ecstasies of a very peculiar kind. To quote Dingwall: "The very word 'love' used to throw her in a state of rapture, and it is said that she used to run about in the nunnery calling out that word in a state of frenzied excitement. The fire by which she was consumed was difficult to slake, so she used to drink quantities of very cold water, bathed her face and arms in it, and throw down her dress in order to cool her breasts. Sometimes also she would seize an image of the Saviour and, removing all her clothes and ornaments, would declare that she would have him naked, so that she might be reminded of all his virtues just as he was, a naked child. Then she used to cry out over and over again: 'O Lord, my God, it is enough, it is enough, it is too much, O Jesus ... O God of Love, no, I can never stop from crying of love, O, you my love, the joy of my heart, the hope and the consolation of my soul ...' Finally in a paroxysm of frenzy she used to cry: 'O love, thou art melting and dissolving my very being. Thou art consuming me and killing me ... O come, come, and love, love!' "

It is not difficult to imagine that at a moment like that orgasm was reached. Yet the saint's desires were not all satisfied: "Sometimes her fevered imagination and the sexual torments to which she was subjected, and which

23

were doubtless sharpened by her perverse passion for flagellation and beating herself with nettles, conjured up before her every kind of lascivious thought and lewd spectacle, until, driven almost to frenzy, she would rush out into the garden, and there, pulling off her tunic, she would roll naked on thorns and then return, but only to whip herself until the blood ran. Or, again, she would have herself tied up and blindfolded in order, so she said, that her body might be still further mortified.

"Another of her notions was to have herself whipped by the prioress in the presence of the other nuns, and now and then others were called in to slap and spank her. Or she would imagine she was an animal and play around on the ground picking up pieces of bread with her teeth, or she would lie down and get the other nuns to walk over her. Then she used to crawl about under the table with a coil of rope round her neck and kiss the feet of the nuns, or maybe have herself tied up to a post demanding insults and gibes of every kind."

In most of the big city-brothels which have existed during the last century or so the interests of people like St Mary Magdalene de Pazzi have been provided for, the purely sexual nature of the whippings and humiliations they required having been recognised. However, several centuries ago, women like this remarkable nun were so uncommon in their desires that one thought them to be unworldly saints.

As the true nature of St Mary Magdalene de Pazzi's taste in penance was not recognised, it is understandable that female homosexuals could live and love in nunneries without being found out. Simple-minded women who had taken the vow of chastity but were troubled by erotic desires turned to each other. As long as their virginity stayed intact, no man came into play and consequently there was no reason for jealousy on the part of their "heavenly bridegroom", thus nobody thought about sins being committed.

24

And nobody cared.

This statement is not as bold as it sounds. People never took female homosexuality very seriously. Even in the Talmud of the ancient Hebrews—a source of much intolerance—lesbianism was regarded as an unimportant sin, the consequence of which was exclusion from marriage with a priest. On the contrary male homosexuality was regarded as a capital sin and subject to capital punishment. It was the loss of sperm that made the Hebrews irreconcilable in regard to male homosexuality and masturbation. The reason of that conduct was clear: the Messiah was expected. He had to be born out of woman and to be begotten by man —hence every irresponsible loss of sperm could be disastrous and was to be regarded as the breaking of a divine law.

The Bishop of Worms laid down punishments in his canonical laws against tribadism, yet in general the conduct of lesbian inmates of nunneries was unnoticed. As soon as perversions were committed for religious reasons mediaeval man accepted them—even cherished them. The repression of these acts was only a façade; a kind of etiquette to hide the realities of life. In this spiritual climate lesbianism flowered. The inmates of the nunneries took to each other for want of men and because of the vow they had taken.

From this period we in fact know only of one case where a legal indication of a certain lesbian act was later on proved in reality. Though there exists a French law forbidding the use of artificial phalli in nunneries, attaching to this delict an imprisonment of seven years, further practical data were at one time unforthcoming.

About 1850, however, an artificial penis was discovered (and confiscated) in an Austrian nunnery. Friedrich Krauss, one of the pioneers of sexual anthropology, describes it in the following way: "This member consists of a tube, narrowing at the end; it is about ten inches long and has an average diameter of one and three-quarter inches. At both ends the ridges are thickened and carved, with the obvious

25

purpose of increasing the friction when using it. The outside is decorated with obscene carvings: a vagina, an erected member and a naked man, a steatopyge type, with his member in full erection. The inside of the tube was filthy from old talcum powder."[2]

As the later Middle Ages do not produce any notable change in the attitude of the worldly and clerical authorities towards female homosexuality, we wish to be brief about this period. Still as a convincing proof that during these years lesbian love existed, on a somewhat smaller scale, we should like to quote a passage from Sir Philip Sidney's bucolic romance *The Arcadia* where he says, in reference to two princesses who are going to sleep: "The bed looked so beautiful because of the wonderful dresses they [the princesses] wore, that it even surpassed on that night the beauty of the bed of Venus. The women embraced each other tenderly and exchanged their passionate kisses. It looked as if Amor let them make love *without the use of his arrow....*"[3]

THE LESBIAN SCENE IN MORE RECENT CENTURIES

The Reformation came and suddenly the whole scene changed. Religious ecstasy became a forbidden word. Man came down to earth. The agony and ecstasy of mediaeval religion was gone, but the Christian ethics stayed the same. It was no longer possible to get around them by way of religious experience. Instead of a society whose freedom was guaranteed by its childlike naïvety, a new society was created. Its members were divided into people who defied the newly imposed morals and people who resigned themselves to their fate.

In most cases it was the nobility that rebelled. The ordinary man felt protected by the moral dogmas and looked indignantly at the conduct of his betters who trampled upon Christian ethics, knowing he could not stop them. For it had not been such a long time since he still had been a serf. Now he was free, he had a roof over his head and had to be contented. As for the new morality that was enforced upon him, he had to make the best of it.

It is in the first group, that of the rebelling nobility, that we find the great lesbians of the time. Lesbianism moved out of the nunneries and into the palaces. It did not only change its surroundings: it also changed its character. For the first time lesbianism became a forbidden pleasure. Wealthy women, bored by their husbands and lovers, fell for something new. It was Paris that became the capital of lesbianism and it was to this city that women flocked to eat from the forbidden fruit and gain a knowledge, that was as old as mankind, but was now outlawed and consequently much more attractive.

Though it does not produce the abundance of material the eighteenth century shows, still the seventeenth century offers already far more facts about sapphism than the sixteenth century. It has become the age of the *chroniqueurs* and as a source of reliable information these are invaluable.

Brantôme gives an elaborate description of homosexuality between women in the first chapter of his *Vie des Dames Galantes*, while Hamilton, who has given us a most witty and lively picture of the debaucheries of court life under the reign of Charles II in his *Memoirs of the Life of Count Grammont* (Hamilton's brother-in-law!) narrates in full detail how Miss Hobart, one of the King's favourites and notorious because of her lesbian tendencies, tries to seduce (and apparently succeeds) the lovely young Miss Temple. Karl Ulrichs in his *Prometheus* cites the scandalous life of Mademoiselle de Maupin, the famous opera-singer and woman fencer who used to shock Paris with her exuberant and shameless ways of transvestitism, nevertheless ending her life quietly in a nunnery.

We even find a royal example of lesbianism during this period in the personality of Queen Christina of Sweden

27

(1626–1689), whose negative attitude to male lovers, preference for transvestitism, and friendship with the Countess Ebba Sparre, were no secret to the public. In the eighteenth century female homosexuality for the first time after classical antiquity reaches a real zenith, especially at the end of this century in France, under the better-class bourgeoisie and in the court circles. There is no period in the history of lesbian love about which we are better informed.

Apart from the revelations by chroniclers like Dulaurens, who wrote a most cynical commentary on the sexual ethics of the Bible, and Chevrier or Piron—all of them getting more and more audacious as the feeling of social and political unrest grew—we find in the overwhelming mass of libels and pamphlets written against both monarchy and clergy, all those factual details we hardly could trace during the Middle Ages. A medical scholar like Tissot states:[3] "We often have seen women loving girls with the same passion men do; we even have noticed how extremely jealous these women get, when their girls are loved by others," and acknowledged and introduced with this statement the *psychological* element in tribadism, as up till then the greater majority of doctors (Duval, Venette for instance) had seen lesbian women only as a special kind of hermaphrodite. Tissot mentions the means by which the lesbians fulfilled their sexual desires too, and speaks in this respect of "masturbation clitoridienne". Aronsson goes even further, and flatly states to have witnessed that lesbian acts between little girls from seven to eight years old regularly happen. He says:[4] "It sounds unbelievable that there are girls from seven to eight years who possess that [lesbian] tendency already in such a way, that while they are sexually still incapable, they still try to find satisfaction in the most unnatural ways. The pity is, this is all too true. I have found those early ripe servants of lewdness too often in the bigger towns."

Before we illustrate this special episode in French and lesbian history with a few famous cases, after which we

28

shall sketch the parallel situation in England, we first want to mention now as the equivalent of the seventeenth-century royal lesbian Queen Christina, the Russian Empress Catherine the Second. In a book[5] published in 1802 containing secret information about Russia, in particular about the last episode of the reign of Catherine II and the accession to the throne of Paul I, we read that Catherine, despite her fabulous heterosexual love-life, finally had become so masculine both in behaviour and taste that she simply had to get women as lovers. As her favourite pets the book names the Princesses Daschkow and Protasow. As further typical evidence for Catherine's sapphism we can add the *ukase* issued on her instigation by the Senate in 1785 which *ukase* advises the courts to judge the cases concerning sodomy "with the utmost clemency and mercy" because "the victims [sic!] must be considered to have been more temporarily out of their wits, than really criminal" At the same time this empress, the friend of Voltaire and other "enlightened philosophers", advised her executioners to use the knout with more severity than they undoubtedly had already done, so we think this woman to be a striking example of the truth that the sadistic element is sometimes to be found either in the background or even as the final motive of lesbian behaviour.

FRENCH COURT CIRCLES A HOTBED OF LESBIANISM

As we have said when starting with this period, the end of the eighteenth century was in respect of erotics in general and sapphism in particular an exact duplicate of classical antiquity. Though the streets of Paris too knew their lesbian women, who looked after the pleasure of voluptuousness in all its manifestations, still one can get the best picture of the atmosphere of this epoch by looking at the court circles, as these represent the best example of the lewdness of those days.

The centre of our attention shall be focussed on Marie

Antoinette, wife of Louis XVI, that gentle but impotent man, and daughter of the famous Empress of Austria, Maria Theresa, who despite the nimbus of piety surrounding her, was an outspoken, shrewd and immoral personality, and quite conscious of the lesbian character of her daughter (see the letter written by Cardinal de Rohan, once an ambassador at Vienna, to Louis XV). The facts about the sapphic affairs of Marie Antoinette, apart from contemporary correspondences, mainly derive from Dreux du Radier's memoirs.[6] After her flighty affair with actresses like Sophie Arnould,[7] Louise Clairon and the famous Guimard, Marie Antoinette encounters her first lesbian love in the figure of Princess de Lamballe. About the time of their meeting de Lamballe was twenty-five; though she was gay, she was not very witty and had some quite childish mannerisms; the sight of a lobster made her swoon with ecstasy, but at the same time she often had nervous breakdowns followed by fainting fits, twice a week and always on the same days and hours. According to her physician, those fits were the sheer consequence of her masturbational excesses. Though the affair between the two women was public knowledge, the King did not object, because his wife had assured him that the pleasures she shared with de Lamballe at the Petit Trianon, happened *without the assistance of any man*. Of these pleasures we find the following description in an anonymously published little book[8]: "Then suddenly Marie Antoinette cried ecstatically: 'Oh you rascal, how clever you are in the art of amusing your sex. How mobile your fingers are! How elastic is your tongue! Arnould is nothing compared with you. You reunite in your personality divers talents of all tribades, past and present. If men were one day to abandon us, we could hardly be pitied, seeing that we know so well how to replace them.'" But Marie Antoinette's feelings were not very stable and so the "unique rascal" was soon thrown away. The Princess de Lamballe however stayed in love with the Queen, and even tried to re-establish their

30

lesbian contacts when Marie Antoinette was imprisoned in the Temple. When reading about the horrible way in which the body of the Princess was mutilated before she was finally killed, one gets the feeling that via her association with the Queen, the public took in this mutilation more a revenge on Marie Antoinette than on the unfortunate de Lamballe herself, and one can only pity the poor woman the more.

Her second real lesbian love Marie Antoinette experienced in the figure of the Countess Jules de Polignac, who thanks to her numerous and lascivious sapphic affairs with nearly all women of her class, undoubtedly can be called the most celebrated lesbian of the eighteenth century. But while the sentiments de Lamballe had cherished for the Queen had been sincere, the feelings of de Polignac were entirely false. The libels and pamphlets written against her pointed out in the most cutting way that de Polignac only had this lesbian relationship with the Queen to gain her social and financial purposes. As de Polignac was a born actress, and played both the sentimental and bestial roles with the greatest naturalness, the Queen had not the slightest idea that the heavenly transports she was raised to were completely staged. Still even the Countess was not able to supply the multiple pleasures her insatiable mistress demanded. In one of her letters to the Abbot of Vermont (about whom she later would say "I whip him, harness him, and ride him"), she complains: "I am believed to be the instigator of everything, whereas in reality I am nothing but a poor pleasure-agent . . . It is no light matter trying continually to please the Queen. You can imagine how difficult it is to lend oneself to all her tastes and to fix her to one pleasure. She wants to pass all in review, and at one and the same instant." In this same letter we find a reference to the King's impotence in relation to the Queen's lesbianism: "It is partly owing to him that the Queen has nearly always preferred the embraces of her own sex to the enjoyments she sought for and expected to find in men".

31

which reference corresponds in a most obvious way with the Queen's own opinion as given in one of her letters to de Polignac: "He [the King] has tonight taken upon himself to embrace me, and give me proof of his love. The proof was but small, but that did not astonish me. I am used to it. What an enormous weight. What a good hammer he would make, but it is a pity the nail is not of stronger steel. I always leave him in a state of desire which sets me on fire. . . ." And as even de Polignac could not extinguish this fire, she was cast off in the same way as de Lamballe had been.

Alphonse Donatien Marquis de Sade, that depraved chronicler of an age of scandal, time and time again mentions in his books secret societies of lesbians and describes their gatherings and the debaucheries the members took part in. In a later chapter dealing with lesbianism in literature, something will be said about the descriptions Sade gives. Now it is important to state that the "Divine Marquis" wrote true to facts. He only put on paper things that happened in his time and his surroundings and to people he knew[9].

AN ARISTOCRATIC LESBIAN SECT

When Sade writes about lesbian secret societies he means clubs like the "Anandryne Sect". Members met in their "Temple of Vesta" and called themselves "pupils of the true Goddess of Love". Another French author and contemporary of Sade was Mairobert. In his *L'Espion Anglais*[10] he wrote a *Confession d'une Jeune Fille*. This text is a true account of a young girl who was admitted to this famous secret society of lesbians of eighteenth-century Paris.

The girl, Mairobert calls her Mademoiselle Sappho, was born in the village of Villiers-le-Bel and was the daughter of a farmer. When she was fifteen she already had a very passionate character and was "in the habit of undressing

32

and masturbating in front of a mirror".[11] When her mother one day caught her in the act, she left home and asked a Madame Gourdan, who exploited the Villiers-le-Bel branch of a Parisian brothel, for work.

Madame Gourdan sent the girl to an assistant who trained would-be prostitutes. It was this woman who wrote her after some days the following letter:

"This child is a real treasure. I give you my word that she is still a virgin. More important is that she has a truly diabolic clitoris. I think that makes her more suitable for women than for men. Our renowned tribades will give you pure gold for this new acquisition."

In eighteenth-century France girls with a large clitoris were very much sought after. Garnier states that a friend of his examined a girl whose clitoris had a length of almost seven inches. That record was surpassed by a girl who owned a clitoris that had a length—again according to Garnier—of one foot! The importance of such a remarkably well-developed clitoris is understandable if one reads in Sade's *Juliette* about a twenty-year-old tribade, Madame de Volmar, who had a clitoris of three and a half inches which made it possible for her "to play the part of a man and a pederast".

Before knowing what Madame Gourdan did with her precious "new acquisition" it is interesting to know a little more about the Parisian head branch of her brothel. It was situated in the Rue des Deux Portes and during the reign of Louis XV and Louis XVI was regarded as the most famous and most refined brothel in the world. It was visited only by members of the royal household and important foreign visitors, and consisted of several sections that all played an important part in the satisfaction of the visitors' sexual passions. The "Serail" was the name for a large hall. Twelve girls were here on duty day and night. They received visitors, catered to their wishes and here, in this big room, the price of the desired performance was agreed upon and details of the desired orgies were given. In the "Piscine" the girls of Madame Gourdan bathed and perfumed their bodies. Here false maidenheads were installed and here was kept the supply of *Essence à l'usage des monstres*—a love potion with a very penetrating smell that made potent the impotent customers and stimulated "monsters" to atrocities.

The next room was the "Cabinet de Toilette" where novices were trained. The "Salle de Bal" was a room that was connected by a secret door with the house of a merchant in the Rue Saint-Sauceur. It was the entrance for clergymen and judges and in a special room they could dress as soldiers or sailors. In the "Infirmerie" the impotent could regain their sexual powers. Here was a small library of obscene books and prints, perfumed rods were used for flagellation and coloured dragées were served that restored sexual power within a few minutes. In this room was a bed covered with black silk. The ceiling and the walls were covered by mirrors which reflected everything that happened in the "Infirmerie" to the visitor who occupied the bed with the girl of his choice. The "Chambre de la Question" was situated in the centre of the house and was visited by voyeurs. In the walls were peep-holes that made it possible to see the occurrences in the other rooms without being seen. The "Salon de Vulcan" had a "torture chair". A girl who sat down in it was automatically fastened by a trap. The back of the chair bent backwards and within a few seconds she lay in a helpless position.

The proprietor of this house was very pleased with the young girl from Villiers-le-Bel and sent the following letter to Madame de Furiel, one of the most famous lesbians of Paris:

Madame,
   I've discovered for you a subject worth a king, or better: worth a queen. I know your generosity and this is to let you know that I have at your service the

most wonderful clitoris in France, a young virgin of fifteen years. Try her and I'm sure you will not know how to express your gratitude. If you're not pleased you can send her back to me—but only if she hasn't suffered too much in your hands. I think I can still surprise the connoisseurs among my clients with a magnificent virgin.

Yours truly,

Gourdan

The deal took place and Mademoiselle Sappho was sold for one hundred louis d'or to Madame de Furiel. De Furiel was a dark haired woman of thirty-two with a very masculine appearance. She initiated Sappho in the secrets of lesbianism and introduced her to the members of the famous "Secte Anandryne". The members of this secret society met, as already mentioned, in the "Temple of Vesta", a large building that contained hundreds of reliefs and statues. In one room there were obscene pictures and statues picturing heterosexual scenes. Novices had to be in this room for three hours, three days in a row. They had to feed two fires with a special fuel, that was very quickly consumed by the flames. As soon as their attention wandered to the surrounding images of men and their monstrous members, the fire extinguished. If this happened the novice was refused admittance.

Madame de Furiel introduced her love slave in this circle of lesbians. The girl had to undress and was then examined by those present to discover how many of the thirty charms of women, described in an old French poem by Jean de Nevizan, she possessed. The poem[12] was read by one of the members of the society.

To be admitted to the "Secte Anandryne" the novice had to possess at least sixteen of these thirty charms. Each pair of tribades decided separately. The opinions were whispered in the ear of the lady president who, after counting votes, announced the result.

35

After being admitted Sappho had to repeat the following words, which were recited: "A lesbian is a young maiden who, having had no intercourse with men, is convinced of the excellence of her own sex, finds in it the true and pure kind of love, pledges herself to it completely and renounces the other sex as wicked and perfidious. It is also a woman of any age who, having complied with the laws of nature and the state for the propagation of the human race, is now regretful of her mistake, and now despises and adjures those hateful pleasures and surrenders herself to become one of the pupils of the true Goddess of Love."

The lady president of the "Secte Anandryne" who formulated these words was a remarkable woman who combined business with pleasure. For a very long time Françoise Clairien Raucourt, as her name was, had been the mistress of the Marquis de Bièvre. After having ensured herself of a yearly income of 12,000 livres she left him and founded her lesbian secret society. The Marquis was not amused by the conduct of his ex-mistress and called her "l'Ingrate Amaranthe" (l'ingrate à ma rente).

In eighteenth-century Paris lesbians were not satisfied by being tolerated. They wanted the key positions in the high society of the French capital and they got them. The French Revolution changed everything. Thousands of aristocrats were killed and with them all members of the highly aristocratic "Secte Anandryne". Only Françoise Clairien Raucourt, the lady president, survived. She died in 1815 at the age of 62.

How was the situation in England during those days? Von Archenholtz in his *Britische Annalen*, Vol. 1, writes: "As in London voluptuousness and lewdness have no other limitations than the limitations of possibility, here too we find females who only commit sexual-acts with their own species. This type of women is called 'tribades'. They establish little groups called 'Anandrine societies', wherein they perform their impure acts." The author of *Satan's Harvest Home* (London 1749), refers to tribades

36

too, when he speaks about lesbian women in London, and uses for the sapphic sex-act the expression "game at flats" He emphasises the fact that this "new way of sin" is especially found between women of the better classes, which statement is later confirmed by Hüttner, who says that these practices already start at the boarding-schools. A typical case of transvestite-lesbianism we find cited by Mantegazza in *Anthropologische Studien*, where he narrates how in 1777 a woman was put into prison for six months, as she had, dressed as a man, already married thrice with various women. Though as a phenomenon not directly related to lesbianism, we still want to mention Hermaphroditism or Viraginism in this survey because we encounter many female homosexuals in this category and because to several authors of this period hermaphroditism is a typically English thing. Adrian, an author from the beginning of the nineteenth century, says in this respect: "When one sees two English women walking down the street, one is apt to imagine they are walking to the rhythm of drum-beats and the hollering of military commands." To those Viragines has even been devoted an extremely pornographic book, entitled *Letters from Laura and Eveline; giving an account of their Mock-Marriage, Wedding-Trip, etc.*

Though during the eighteenth century in England lesbianism certainly flourished in the theatre-world, and during that period had close connections with prostitution as well, still we get our first reliable information about these relationships from a nineteenth-century source.[13]

Ellis and Symonds say in this book that passionate friendships between girls, from the most innocent to the most developed ways of lesbian love were often to be encountered in the staff of theatres, including actresses as well as chorus- and ballet-girls. It was nevertheless exceptional for these relationships to go to the ultimate. The English girls from the lower- and middle-classes, whether or not virgins, were entirely dominated by convention. In the

37

upper classes perversity was more practised because those classes were more free to do as they liked and had a more varied set of moral standards. In the same way tribadism existed among the more distinguished courtesans, though between the lower-class street-girls lesbianism was hardly to be found. Such girls as these latter had often never even heard of lesbianism and were shocked when told about it; they considered it belonged to "French bestiality".

In the nineteenth century generally, however, female homosexuality almost disappeared from the scene. Middle-class women were not yet emancipated. Women of the working-class were glad if they had enough to eat for their families and it was only during the industrial revolution when girls left their homes and entered factories that intimate companionships arose, due to the fact that work had to be done under crowded and squalid conditions. To most of these working-class lesbians homosexuality was only an easy way to escape from the dreary, shabby world of everyday life. These girls most of the time were bisexuals who turned to their own sex because their senses were starving and there were not enough men to be found. For this was the age of colonial conquests and in France and England, as well as in Germany, young men were sent to Asia and Africa.

LESBIANISM IN OUR OWN TIME

It is only since the Second World War that lesbianism has made a comeback, almost as powerful as in the eighteenth century. During the war thousands of women who served in the armies, navies and air-forces of England, the United States and Germany, found out they were homosexual. After the war they continued their newly found existence. At the same time the "new morality" that has been sweeping the world and that wants to call a spade a spade caused the publication of countless books

38

and magazines that dealt with aspects of lesbianism. Movies were made about lesbian problems. Lesbians appeared on television and talked about their world and their way of life. Female homosexuality is no longer hushed up. Nor is it considered only as a "thrill" for bored aristocratic women. Nowadays it is seen as a factor that decides the lives of millions of women.

As a consequence of the lesbian's comeback, in every capital of the Western world a great number of bars and amusement centres that are almost exclusively frequented by lesbians can be found. In the East, Tokio is about the only centre of lesbian night-life. In this city a guide brings the tourist to secret theatres where performances of lesbian love-making defy any description. Of course this does not mean that the Japanese lesbian-in-the-street frequents these theatres! The performances are strictly part of the tourist trade. The Japanese lesbians have their own bars in the obscure side-alleys of Tokio's centre of night-life. These bars are quiet places where a tourist would not find anything of interest.

Lesbian bars all over the world have—like bars for male homosexuals—one thing in common. They are quiet. There are no brawls. They are just places were one can see friends and acquaintances, meet people one is interested in and have a drink or two.

In countries where homosexuality is punished by the law the true nature of the "queer bar" is kept secret. After one or two raids by the police the habitués leave and try to find a new meeting-place elsewhere.

In countries where the police have no special interest in homosexuals life is less complicated. There lesbians have their own bars, where heterosexuals are welcome as well, but where the atmosphere is exclusively homosexual.

Antwerp is a well-known centre of homosexuality. Here not only Belgian lesbians frequent the little bars in the neighbourhood of the railway station, but German female homosexuals travel hundreds of miles to spend an evening among their kind. A very well known "queer bar" in Antwerp is situated in an avenue leading to the railway station. Lesbians asking in cafés and restaurants for the address of a lesbian bar are always advised to visit this café. It is a cosy place, where the atmosphere is strictly homosexual.

Of course Paris has a great number of bars and nightspots that cater to a lesbian clientèle. One of the most famous is Frede Carroll's, in Rue Sainte-Anne, off the Avenue de l'Opera. Miss Frede is smartly dressed in masculine attire and her partner in management is a very beautiful and feminine American woman named Miki. There is hot music for bachelor-girls and their friends, and for those of the male sex who come to watch.*

In the years between 1920 and 1933 Berlin was the world's capital of homosexuality. Homosexual bars advertised in the daily papers and were a part of everyday life. There were bars for male and for female homosexuals. In both of them men and women transvestites were to be found. An unsuspecting heterosexual visitor to one of these meeting-places often could not see what was so special about the place as the number of "male" and "female" visitors seemed to balance. The most famous of these homosexual bars in pre-Hitler Berlin was the "Eldorado" in the Motzstrasse.

Nowadays homosexuality in Germany is frowned upon and German as well as English homosexuals flock to a new homosexual Eden. In the 'sixties Amsterdam became the Mecca for the world's homosexuals. There are more than twenty "gay" bars at this moment and two homosexual clubs that both have thousands of members.

The owner of a well-known and very picturesque bar at the Zeedijk is one of the city's best-known lesbians. Every night she and her friend serve at the bar. The bar is an attraction for sailors, students and lesbians who feel perfectly at home in each other's company. Lesbians who want to

* See *Paris by Night* by Jacques Robert. London, Charles Skilton, 30/-.

spend a pleasant and not too expensive evening in Amsterdam can go to a bar near the Leidsestraat, a place that advertises itself with the slogan "for friends only". Of course there are many others that are frequented exclusively by homosexuals. Then there is the show the boys put on in the Madame Arthur, a night-club where men dressed and made-up as women dance and sing—many an unsuspecting heterosexual visitor from outside the city falls for one of the "girls". The audience, however, includes also quite a sprinkling of women, many in pairs.

At two o'clock all the bars close for the night. Then the gay boys and girls go to the Dok, a club for homosexuals that is situated in the gigantic cellars of an auction-room at the Singel, right in the heart of the town. This club closes at four o'clock and on Saturdays and Sundays at five in the morning. Here one can drink and dine, dance and listen to the music. Some of the performers from Madame Arthur reappear here. Every night hundreds of male and female homosexuals enter the club, just to spend an evening or to find a pick-up. On the dance floor romantic couples swoon. The club is visited by many well-known artistes and actors who make no secret of their interests. Foreign visitors can enter the premises on presentation of their passport. On Saturday nights and at Christmas and Easter the club is crowded with visitors from Germany and England. Every spring there is a big carnival-party with everybody dressing up and trying to steal the show.

The Dok is one Amsterdam club for homosexuals. The C.o.c is another one. This club, situated near the amusement centre of the Leidseplein, is much more sophisticated and culturally minded than the Dok. At the C.o.c one can drink and dance, but one can also hear lectures on subjects of interest to homosexuals. The C.o.c publishes its own magazine *Dialoog*, a bi-monthly one can buy at the news-stands. One of the main ends of the C.o.c is the integration of homosexuals into a heterosexual society. At this moment

41

in all big cities of Holland welfare centres for homosexuals are found.

In the United States each summer lesbians meet at Fire Island, a summer resort with an exclusively homosexual clientèle. Fire Island is situated about forty miles from New York and only a few miles south of Long Island. We find there a small society of cottages where lesbian couples spend their vacations. Many of the cottages bear names that hint at the activities their inhabitants take part in. The most colourful I noticed while doing some research at Fire Island were: "Sinerama", "Les Girls" and "The Hothouse".

One of the strangest phenomena in lesbianism is the international fraternity that seems to exist between homosexual women in different countries. Many lesbians are always on the go, restlessly travelling from one big city to another, forever crossing frontiers and meeting new friends, starting relationships that most of the time turn out to be only one-night stands. I noticed most of these girls knew names and addresses of contacts in other parts of the world. A few of them even had their little black books, crammed with names and addresses of notorious lesbian prostitutes in the big cities of France, Germany, England and Sweden. They all knew where they could find "the girls" in cities as distant as Stockholm, Copenhagen, London, Brussels and Amsterdam. I asked them who gave them these names and addresses.

"Nobody," one of them said. "They are very easy to collect as soon as you know of the existence of a lesbian grapevine. You just have to listen carefully to what others say. Then you'll always know what's going on in the lesbian scene in New York, London or Paris."

In every big city nowadays there is one older lesbian who acts as a source of information for girls who are willing to travel and see the world. She hands them information about clubs, bars and lesbians in the city the girl wants to go to. A girl I interviewed told me about a real "lesbian

42

vade-mecum" who knew people and places in such far-away places as the South American republics.

"She has it all in her card-index," the girl told me. "If you want information about, say, lesbian hotels in Singapore, just go to her and she will tell you. Of course I don't know if you, being a man, will have to pay for it. To us she charges nothing..."

NOTES

1. Dr E. J. Dingwall wrote two amusing books: *Human Oddities* and *Very Peculiar People*, both published in London. The story of St Mary Magdalene de Pazzi can be found in *Some Human Oddities*.

2. *Anthropophyteia*, Vol. 3.

3. Tissot, *L'onanisme, dissertation sur les Maladies Produites par la Masturbation*, 1768.

4. I. E. Aronsson, *Die Kunst, das Leben des schönen Geschlechts zu verlängeren, seine Schönheit zu erhalten und es in seinen eigentümlichen Krankheiten vor Missgriffen zu bewahren*. Berlin 1806.

5. *Geheime Nachrichten von Russland*, 1802.

6. Dreux du Radier, *Mémoires historiques et anecdotes sur des Reines et Régentes de France*, 1827.

7. See *La nouvelle Sapho ou histoire de la Secte Anandryne* by La C. R. 1791.

8. *The day of love, or the last pleasures of M . . . A . . .* (No date).

9. This was proven in detail by Dühren in his book *Der Marquis de Sade und seine Zeit*, Berlin, several editions. Dühren also discovered the manuscript of Sade's most famous book: *The 120 days of Sodom*. This book was published in an English translation by the Olympia Press of Paris.

10. Mairobert is a famous and reliable chronicler of the morals of his contemporaries.

11. Quoted by Hirschfeld in *Die Homosexualität des Mannes und des Weibes*, p. 78. Actually we do not think that this is any proof of a "very passionate character". The author must have known very little of the activities of fifteen-year-old girls.

12. The poem is printed in translation, with some other details, in *Female Homosexuality*, by Frank S. Caprio, New York 1954, London 1957.

13. Havelock Ellis and J. A. Symonds, *Sexual Inversion*, London 1897.

CHAPTER THREE

Lesbianism in the East and Africa

"She used to compel the young male slaves to mount her, and she herself loved to mount the young female slaves . . . she was terribly expert in the titillant art."

That is the way a lesbian is described in the *Arabian Nights*.[1] We know lesbianism has always been a common thing in the East. As a matter of fact most of the lesbians in Eastern and African countries are bisexuals. As the greatest part of them live together in harems and share one husband, the only way of getting sexual gratification regularly is by mutual masturbation. These women choose friends among the members of a harem, friends that act as partners in lesbian love-play, and they stay faithful to their lover. Anthropologists have witnessed dramatic scenes of jealousy between lovers in a harem.

In the Orient an artificial penis is much more used during love-play than in Western countries. Lesbians can purchase these instruments without embarrassment and most of the times these artificial members are, as one anthropologist describes them, "made of india-rubber of the size and shape of an erect penis perforated longitudinally and fitted with warm water or milk, so that by squeezing it, an ejaculation can be counterfeited. It can also be attached to the body by means of a girdle and can thus be employed for the gratification of another individual".

The description of lesbian practices in the *Arabian Nights* dates back many ages, and we now wish to give a short résumé of lesbian love-life in those countries which

44

made history until the moment that the world's entire fate was laid in the hands of Western European power.

Apart from all the anecdotes existing about sapphism in harems, brothels, court- and temple-circles, one of the striking indications that lesbianism was known in Egypt can be found in the personality of Queen Hatschepsut, who reigned for more than twenty years. On the statues erected to honour her, she is never represented as a woman, but always as a man. Even the little fake beard (*spitzen- bart*) of the Pharaohs, has not been forgotten, and only the inscriptions on the monument reveal the identity of her sex. It is hardly amazing in this respect that the historian Erman compares her with the lesbian Catherine II of Russia. In the *History of Egypt* Breasted calls her the first important woman history has had.

Already Herodotus mentions, when speaking about Babylon and Assyria, female temple prostitution "in the unnatural direction". As we can judge by the famous laws of the Emperor Hammurabi, here too, as in Rome, there were no legal sanctions against sexual intercourse between women. Though there does not exist absolutely reliable data about the lesbian character of the Assyrian Queen Semiramis, nevertheless her behaviour towards her ministers and generals (whom she led through nine wars) makes her to our opinion an equivalent of Queen Hatschepsut.

In Phoenicia, too, the simple historical fact of the Astarte-cult and its female prostitution proves the exist- ence of a lesbian love-life. (The Phoenician women had the reputation of painting their vaginal-lips in imitation of the entry to the sanctuary of love.) In Phoenicia's colony Car- thage the same pattern existed, though undoubtedly the relationship between their leaders Hasdrubal and Hannibal make this to the general public more a typical example of a male-homosexual community (See Pietschman[2] and Livy, caput 21).

Though Central Arabia has been the cradle of the Middle

East—where, as we have shown, tribadism was quite a normal thing—still in respect of Arabia itself only the female temple prostitution ("in the unnatural direction" here too) attached to the cult of the Goddess Ma or Kybele hints that sapphism might have existed there, though according to Ploss, the natural length of the clitoris of oriental women was of such extraordinary dimensions that sexual intercourse between women nearly became a natural consequence.

At the periphery of the Middle East lived the Scythians and Tartars, and though we nowhere discovered any factual information about lesbian relationships there, nevertheless the description given by Hippocrates of the characteristics of Scythian women (they fulfilled the duties usually performed by men, such as hunting, horse-riding, military service etc.) is in such complete accordance with the picture given by Herodotus about the Amazons—a people supposed to be lesbian—that we think it highly probable that between the Scythian women sexual intercourse did exist.

As the material about the Amazons generally does not surpass the level of legend, we want to cite in this respect the proposition of one of the best-informed scholars about homosexuality, Karsch-Haack[3], who does not treat—like Herodotus logically did—the Amazons as a *people*, as a geographically defined entity with certain specific characteristics, psychologically explicable, because of local circumstances, but sees the Amazons as a *phenomenon*, regularly happening where certain inescapable predispositions simply force it to happen. As soon as the exclusively male character of society either weakens or gradually vanishes—whatever the reasons may be—women leave the background they have been kept in, and start sharing the typical male activities, while—for instance with the Scythians—the men start performing the duties up till then performed by women, and the phenomenon "Amazon", the "free-" female, who is out for all she has missed during

46

ages, is born. And when the past has not already created it, the new situation will bring forth the contempt of man and that contempt simply makes the female destined for lesbian love. Because of this Karsch-Haack states that the widespread Amazon-myths—(many of them to be found amongst the Malayans and the negroes in the Congo, where according to Reade's *Savage Africa* (1863) lived "a female Napoleon, Queen Shinga" who after having lost her empire to the Portuguese during three fierce battles, even recaptured it in 1646 and reigned over it for quite another long period of time)—are of the utmost importance for the history and explanation of sexual intercourse between women.

Between the Middle and Far East, India is situated, and though only one of the many oriental countries, still the average laymen identifies the whole of the Orient mostly with this country as far as sex matters are concerned, because of the world-wide reputation of Vatsyayana's *Kama Sutra*.* We quite agree with the high esteem this book generally enjoys, still one wonders that only a few passages are devoted to sapphism, though perhaps this is a natural consequence of a society so entirely dominated by man. Nevertheless ample proof of lesbian love is found in the following statement of Vatsyayana: "The women of the royal harem cannot see or meet any men on account of their being strictly guarded, neither do they have their desires satisfied, because their only husband is common to many wives. For this reason among themselves they give pleasure to each other in various ways as now described.

"Having dressed the daughters of their nurses, or their female friends, or their female attendants, like men, they accomplish their object by means of bulbs, roots, and fruits having the form of the Lingam, or they lie down upon the statue of a male figure in which the Lingam is visible and erect."

* The illustrated paperback edition is published by Luxor Press at 9/6.

47

The same things we find mentioned by Yasodhara. Régla[4], however, states explicitly that lesbian love was in the Middle and Far East certainly not restricted to seraglios, and describes circumstantially how the younger girls were instructed by the older ones in lesbian practices while using at the same time drugs like hashish or belladonna. The final proof of the existence of sexual intercourse between women outside the harem are the statues of goddesses like Pudicitia and Bona Dea who were specially honoured by female homosexuals; Metha in his *Scientific Curiosities of Sex Life* is of the opinion that during the ritual attached to the cult of these goddesses, artificial male members were used.

Since the Far East offers such an immense variety of populations, and as dealing with most of these countries would bring this survey out of proportion to the rest of the book, we shall describe only some examples of sapphism in Siam and in the Indonesian Archipelago, as these cases are rather original on the one hand, while producing on the other hand definite proof of the existence of female homosexuality in these parts of the world.

The example in Siam, narrated by Jan Mocquet in his *Itinerarium*, although rather horrid, leaves no doubt of a lesbian love-life there. For though this particular case refers to sexual circumstances in a harem, we think in complete accordance with Régla that as soon as tribadism reveals itself somehow, it does exist in all its aspects within that specific society. Mocquet describes the following scene: "When a certain King of Siam had been informed that his concubines, the most beautiful girls of the country, fulfilled their sexual lusts between each other by imitating the masculine way of fornication by means of an artificial penis, he decided to have every woman guilty of this behaviour branded on the forehead and cheeks with a piece of metal representing the masculine sex-organ, after which treatment these women were burned alive."

Of the islands of the Indonesian Archipelago, Bali is in respect to our subject the most interesting one. Of course we do meet female homosexuality on the other isles of the Archipelago as well. Julius Jacobs[5] mentions that in Atjeh (on Sumatra) tribadism between older girls by means of a *dilin* (i.e. a male member made of wax) is no rarity. Perelaer[6] explains the low birth-rate of the people on Borneo by pointing at the extremely high scale of sexual intercourse between women of this country.

Van Brero has given a most exclusive example of sapphism in his book[7] published in 1897, in which he describes that among some women living in the Eastern part of Java he has met specimens of *born* lesbians, who from their earliest childhood onwards show these tendencies in imitating the habits of the male sex in every aspect, for instance dress, games, attitude. These women were called by the rest of the population *wandu* which means hermaphrodite; curiously enough the same expression is used for the male homosexual as well.

However interesting these examples may be, still the Isle of Bali, as said above, is for the history of lesbianism and for the description of its practices far more important than the other isles of the Archipelago. The literature about Bali is fairly extensive and at the same time extremely precise in the details it gives of the female homosexual act. Julius Jacobs, an authority in the field of indology, states elsewhere[8] that the scale on which tribadism was practised there did not differ from the scale on which male homosexuality was practised. The word used for the lesbian sex-act is *metjengtjeng djoeoek* meaning literally "to let the pelvises beat against each other in such a way that no sound can be heard". To Jacobs this way of sexual intercourse between women is the real lesbian act, though he adds that the digital and lingual variations exist also. It is his firm opinion that the extremely well-developed clitoris

49

of the Balinese women—a fact acknowledged by many authors—though it did not exactly predispose them to sapphism, certainly stimulated their eventual latent lesbian tendencies. On Bali too, according to Jacobs, the women living in harems, possessed their artificial wax-made male members, *tjelak-tjelakan malem*—which the *vox populi* called *koempentji*, the substitute, while the poorest type of tribades used in this respect the *pisang*, the banana.

As a most sensational phenomenon Jacobs mentions that on Bali existed a little industry, producing all sorts of art objects, representing the numerous variations of sexual life, but *mainly* either male homosexual and masturbation acts or purely sapphic ways of intercourse. The reasons for the widespreadness of lesbian love-life on Bali Jacobs does not touch on. From other sources, however, like the author van der Tuuk, we know that various aspects of tribadism were incorporated both in the religion itself and in the cult attached to it, and this brings us in complete disagreement with Stoll,[9] who states that both religion and ritual decay as soon as lesbian love starts to flourish. As we have seen on Bali and as we have already encountered in many cases during this survey the clitoris has been of utmost importance for sexual intercourse between women.

In the literature about female homosexuality exist two main schools of thought: one defends the principle that lesbians are born, the other states that lesbianism is acquired. The last-mentioned are partly of opinion that sapphism can be caused by specific particularities of the female sex-organs, and they do not only believe that an over-developed clitoris may be the origin of tribadism, but they think also that the over-developed smaller vaginal lips, the labia minora, are mainly the effect and mostly the proof of lesbian sex acts. The adherents of these theories can cite numerous authors (like Jacobs, for instance) producing examples of a kind which seem to prove the reliability of their trend of thought, although we still have our own doubts. As early as 1753 Parsons mentioned that among the tribes of Asia and Africa the over-developed clitoris was a common thing; in this respect he especially points to the people of Angola. De Graaf however states that the surgical shortening or complete removal of these enormous clitores (macroclitoridae) was even customary with these people, "not only to make sexual intercourse with the male possible, but also to prevent 'the evil' of too many sexual acts as well."

Home describes the genitals of a negro girl on Dominica possessing a clitoris of about four inches long, and as thick as the thumb of a grown-up man, and states significantly that though this woman apart from her penis-like instrument had all the further sexual characteristics of a normal woman, "she nevertheless made in her behaviour the impression of being more a male than a female." Virey in his *De la Femme* (1826) shares the opinion of Jacobs, and says "in southern countries it is quite normal to remove the over-developed clitoris because of the evil either stimulated or caused by it."

A CURIOSITY OF ETHNOLOGY

As we have dealt already in this survey with some other cases of extravagantly enlarged clitores in relation to sapphism, we think it appropriate to leave this subject and turn our attention to what the ethnologists have to say about the phenomenon of the over-developed smaller vaginal lips.

Though enlarged labia minora have been recorded among all sorts of primitive races, the truly over-developed smaller vaginal lips have been found mostly with the tribes of the Bushmen and Hottentots. The smaller lips—usually with European women entirely hidden before defloration—hang down between the larger lips, with a length often surpassing seven inches, grown together more or less in such a way

51

that it gave the impression of being a sort of apron. The term "Hottentot-apron" has therefore even become a standard expression in medical literature, when relating to over-developed smaller vaginal lips. As this "apron" had more or less the same colour as the male organ, often new-comers to these countries had the idea of encountering a man, whilst they were in the company of a woman! Virey says that Kolb has been the discoverer of the Hottentot-apron.

Though originally it was our intention to mention only those authors who saw these over-developed lips as a proof of the existence of a lesbian love-life, we should like to cite some other writers as well, since this phenomenon really is rather exceptional. Cuvier (1817) contests the idea that the "apron" had the function of ornament, as he has witnessed Bushwomen so apt in hiding this "apron" that the fact they wore one was only discovered after their death.

Finsch (1880) however takes the opposite view; he narrates how one of the official community functions of the impotent old men of the tribe was the artificial creation of this "apron" as an ornament by constantly pulling and tugging these lips of the little girls. These same old men, states Finsch, had the task of enlarging the clitoris by con-stantly rubbing and licking it; they even used red ants, as the bite of these insects was considered to have an aphro-disiacal effect.

About the origin of the "apron" all sorts of opinions exist and we should like to mention some of them.

Blanchard[10] saw the "apron" as a typical race-symp-tom, in exact proportion with the position the Bushman had in the development of the human race; to him the way the genitals of the Bushwomen were built was similar to the construction of the genitals of the female apes. To Blan-chard this proved that these people had just left the state of animality behind, and the "apron" was just a natural phenomenon. This opinion was shared by Lichtenstein, who thought that though it was a natural thing, yet the

52

over-development started only when the girls had gone through puberty.

Le Vaillant, however, considered the "Bushman's-apron" entirely as an artificial enlargement of the small vaginal lips, caused by rubbing and tugging. He even claimed that some women used for this purpose rather heavy weights, hanging down for more than nine inches between their legs. He makes the curious remark that "the apron makes such a ridiculous impression, that by looking at it, even the most voluptuous man loses his sexual interests."

We do not know if le Vaillant hints with this statement at the eventual lesbian relationship between Bushwomen. According to Cuvier the real purpose of the "apron" is to protect the female against "the act of violence of the male", as the "apron" makes it impossible for a man to perform coitus without the consent and even the assistance of the woman! Again we do not know if Cuvier too might have connected this behaviour with crypto-lesbian tendencies, but according to Fritsch and Winwood Reade the real origin of the "apron" certainly had its foundation in sapphic desires. Both state that the extraordinary development of the smaller vaginal lips was caused either by single or by mutual masturbation. Modern authors like Bartels and Schröder agree with this judgement; they do not think the "Hottentot- or Bushman's-apron" a rarity after all, since in their own practice they have met similar examples of it (which means among modern German women!), but both claim that a phenomenon like this can only be caused by either single or mutual masturbation in the most extravagant ways.

We realise we have paid rather much attention to all this, but as we consider that, as far as the physical aspects of lesbian love are concerned, the state of both the clitoris and the vaginal lips are of primary importance, and since about this last factor only scanty information is given in the current literature of tribadism, we inevitably have to deal with this material at some length in this survey.

We should like to conclude this chapter with a reference to the Isle of Tahiti, as we have found there a unique lesbian phenomenon. The French doctor "Jacobus X——" gives an elaborate description of this peculiarity in his *L'Ethnologie du Sens Génital* (1901), one of the rarer books about perversions in human sex life.

A few years before the Tahiti girls (the Vahiné) had reached their puberty, their education in sex-matters started. Dance-groups of girls were formed, the number varying from eight to twelve persons, under the supervision of older women. The dance, called Timorodee, was not ritualistic at all but simply consisted of an immense variety of voluptuous gestures and movements invented by fertile lascivious minds. During the dancing a sort of dialogue was going on between the girls and their instructresses in the most obscene language (to our way of thinking) explaining the dance, and commentaries and advice were given. As soon as the girls had reached puberty, these dances were forbidden to them, as these girls were expected to practise their learning from then on in reality. It is obvious that as these dances contained, for instance, initiation into the heterosexual copulation act and the practice of cunnilingus, that these girls were predisposed to lesbian sex acts, at the end of their instruction. These "initiation-techniques" had such a reputation that even from other Polynesian isles girls were sent to Tahiti. The only indication in literature about a related phenomenon is found in Born's description of the Kuthid dance performed by the Yap-women on the Caroline Isles. Still, as this dance was done by women and not by the younger girls, we insist on calling the Tahitian Timorodee dance unique in sapphic life.

1. It is a pity that there exists only one reliable version of these wonderful tales. Most editions of the *Arabian Nights* are bowdlerised versions for children. This fragment is taken from the only complete and unexpurgated edition, the one edited by Sir Richard Burton, the nineteenth-century traveller and linguist. The edition is published by the American Burton Society.

2. Pietschman, *Geschichte der Phönikier*, 1889.

3. Karsch-Haack, *Das Gleichgeschlechtliche Leben der Naturvölker*.

4. Paul de Régla, *Les Bas-Fonds de Constantinople*, 1893.

5. Julius Jacobs, *Familie- en Kampongleven op Groot-Atjeh*. (Family and Village-life on Great Atjeh.)

6. Perelaer, *Ethnographical Descriptions of the Dajaks*, 1870.

7. Van Brero, *Einziges über die Geisteskrankheiten der Bevölkerung des Malaïschen Archipel*, 1897.

8. Julius Jacobs, *Eenigen tijd onder de Baliërs. Eene Reisebeschrijving met aantekeningen betreffende Hygiène, Land- en Volkenkunde van de Eilanden Bali en Lombok*. (My time with the Balinese, some notes concerning hygiene and ethnology of the Isles of Bali and Lombok.)

9. Stoll, *Geschlechtsleben in der Völkerpsychologie*.

10. Blanchard, *Étude sur la Stéatopygie et le Tablier des Femmes Boschimanes*, 1883.

CHAPTER FOUR

The Portrayal of Lesbianism in Art
and Literature

After thousands of years of the most refined culinary
specialities it is still possible to devise new recipes and
invent food nobody tasted before. It is possible to compose
new music, to paint pictures nobody saw before. Only in
the domain of sex all possibilities were exhausted many
centuries ago and even of the most bizarre way of making
love one can say with certainty that it has been done before
—probably thousands of times.

No artist can devise new ways of making love. The only
thing authors, poets, sculptors and painters can do is
praise love and love-making in their own ways, at the same
time trying to depict the old techniques in a new, more
refined way.

In the history of art most of the artists who were interested in painting or carving erotic scenes did not want to
go "all the way". That is the reason lesbian love is a much
more favourite subject than male homosexuality, which in
our Western civilisation was frowned upon. Most artists
thought lesbian love scenes less "crude" and much more
charming than scenes which depicted love-making between
men. It is a striking fact that artists who were homosexuals
themselves showed most interest in depicting lesbian love.
Out of a moral resistance against depicting love for their
own sex, they projected their feelings on passionate imagi-
nations of lesbian love-life.

Boucher, Rodin, Huet, Leger, Rubens, Rops, Dégas,

Félon, Toulouse-Lautrec, Greuze, Somoff, Grigorieff, Godal, Maillol, Picasso, Brüning, von Bayros, Klinger and Klimt were only a few artists—heterosexuals and homosexuals—who were fascinated by female homosexuality. One of the most famous lesbian love scenes is the *Fall of Icarus* by Rodin. Another well-known depiction by the same artist is *Lover's Play* in the Rodin Museum in Paris.

NOVELISTS AND THE LESBIAN THEME

When novelists deal with homosexuality they prefer in general the lesbian side of it because it does not inspire that feeling of aversion male homosexuality does, while at the same time it appeals more to the sexual taste of the average male reader. During the nineteenth century the lesbian theme became definitely popular, and there were published a number of masterpieces in which lesbian love plays a role. Balzac for instance often wrote about it and in books like *Seraphita*, *Scenes of Parisian Life* and *Père Goriot* female homosexuality figures. His famous work *Fille aux Yeux d'Or* (The Girl with the Golden Eyes), which was made into a film a few years ago, contains the remark: "The most powerful sentiment in existence is the love women have for each other."

Zola in his *Nana*, Baudelaire in his *Femmes Damnées*, Alphonse Daudet in *Sappho: A Picture of Life in Paris*, and Thomas Hardy in *Desperate Remedies* describe in their own masterly ways the miseries and happiness, the serenity and passions women can inspire in each other. As a quite different type of lesbian novel, the neurotic one, we want to mention de la Vaudère's *Les Demi-Sexes*, in which the heroines "have themselves castrated to escape sexual intercourse with men".

During the eighteenth century there was Diderot's *La Nouvelle Religieuse*, while for Alphonse Donatien Marquis de Sade lesbian love was a popular theme. *Juliette* opens

with a flaming scene of a lesbian orgy in the nunnery of
Panthémont. In a later chapter of the same work Mondor
is spectator of a specially staged lesbian performance.
Clairwil, a lesbian with a violent hate towards men, stages
an orgy with Juliette and four other women. In his book
Justine there is a lesbian scene between Dorothée and
Madame Gernande. The lesbian Séraphine plays an important part in the book. Sade's lesbians are passionate
pederasts. In *Justine* he tells us that they possess not only
masculine passions but also the refined tastes of men . . .
like for instance the taste for sodomy, from which "because it belongs to one of the most delicate, they have
made one of their most heavenly pleasures".

Verlaine in his *Œuvres Libres* wrote a complete cycle of
poems on the subject of "Les Amies". Some of them are
immortal. For instance this one:

> Tendre, la jeune femme rousse
> Que tant d'innocence émoustille
> Dit à la blonde jeune fille
> Ces mots, tout bas, d'une voix douce:
>
> "Sève qui monte et fleur qui pousse,
> Ton enfance est une charmille;
> Laisse errer mes doigts dans la mousse
> Où le bouton de rose brille.
>
> Laisse-moi, parmi l'herbe claire,
> Boire les gouttes de rosée
> Dont la fleur tendre est arrosée,
>
> Afin que le plaisir, ma chère,
> Illumine ton front candide,
> Comme l'aube l'azur timide."

A few years ago in France *L'Histoire d'O* was published.
The remarkable Olympia Press in Paris—famous pub-

lishers of literary, erotic and pornographic books—brought
an English translation on the international market (in most
countries this international market was situated under the
counter of back-street bookshops) and *The Story of O*, a
strange and haunting book, became world-known.

From this book here follows a fragment that gives a
good impression of the working of a lesbian's mind:

"O had a fairly clear idea of what she was looking for
in the young women she pursued. It wasn't at all that she
was seeking to give herself the impression of being on a
par with men, she wasn't trying, by means of masculine
behaviour, to compensate for some female inferiority she
didn't in the slightest feel. Oh yes, she'd once, at twenty,
when she was courting one of her prettiest friends, surprised herself doffing her beret to say hello, standing back
to allow her to go first, and offering a hand to help her get
out of a taxi. Similarly, she wouldn't stand for not paying
her share of the check when she and a female friend went
for some tea in a pastry-shop. She'd kiss her hand and her
mouth too, if possible right in the middle of the street.
But all that amounted simply to behaviour deliberately
designed to shock, to the effects of childishness much more
than to those of conviction. On the other hand, the strong
liking she had for the sweetness of very sweet painted lips
yielding to hers, for the enamelled or pearly flash of
eyes that half close in the subdued light of divans at five
o'clock in the afternoon when the curtains have been
drawn and the lamp on the mantelpiece lit, for voices which
say: Oh, again, for God's sake, once again, for the
well-nigh ineffaceable marine odour which remained on
her fingers, that liking was strong, it was real and it was
profound.

"And keen too was the joy which she derived from
hunting. It was probably not the hunting in itself, amusing
or exciting as it could be, but the perfect freedom she felt
thrill within her when she hunted. She controlled the game,
and she alone (which, with a man, she never did unless it

59

were on the sly). She held the initiative, the conversations
the rendezvous, the kiss depended upon her, even to the
point where she preferred not to receive but to give the
first kiss, and from the time she began to have lovers, she
would just about never allow the girl she was caressing to
caress her. The greater her yearning to see a friend naked
before her eyes, the less she found any cause to take off her
own clothes. Often, she contrived excuses to avoid undressing, said she was cold, that it was the wrong day of the
month.

"(. . .) Nakedness, the body's abandon had overwhelmed
her, and it had seemed to her that her girl-friends had be-
stowed upon her a gift for which she could never make a
commensurate or equivalent return when they simply con-
sented to exhibit themselves naked in a closed room. For
vacation-time nudity, in the sunshine on the beach, left her
quite cold—not at all because it was public, but because
by being public and by not being unconditional it was, in
some greater or lesser degree, protected."

Erotic and pornographic literature swarms with books
in which lesbian love is the main theme. "E.D.", the
famous French pornographer—in everyday life a respected
wine-merchant—wrote several pornographic novels about
lesbianism. The most famous of them are: *Lesbia, maîtresse
d'école*, *La Comtesse de Lesbos ou la nouvelle Gamiani*
and *Lèvres de velours, suite de la Comtesse de Lesbos*[1].

GAMIANI, OR TWO NIGHTS OF EXCESS

Un Été à la Campagne, attributed to the well-known
French author Gustave Droz[2] was another lesbian epic.
However, most famous of them all was the immortal erotic
novel *Gamiani, ou Deux Nuits d'Excès*, (Brussels, 1833)
illustrated with twelve beautiful lithographs by Devéria.
This first edition did not mention any author, but as soon
as the second edition appeared (in Brussels 1835), with the
addition behind the title "By Alcide, baron de M*****"

rumours started that nobody else than the poet Alfred de Musset could have been the author of this piece of sapphic literature. Though a witty critic once said that on those five asterisks the legend of de Musset's authorship has been built, we think it was the preface of this second edition which established his reputation in this respect. The preface indicated that *Gamiani* had been written a little before the Revolution of 1830 by a young poet who had wanted to write an erotic classic not containing any rude or obscene language; a young poet who was highly gifted artistically, but at the same time was a real roué and a drunkard. The preface even pointed out that his favourite alcohol was absinthe. Now, it was well known that de Musset had been an enslaved absinthe-drinker, and about his "debaucheries" we find ample evidence in a letter written by Mérimée to Stendhal (1831). As we said, from there on the authorship of *Gamiani* by de Musset was to most people a certainty, though to many his real motive in publishing it had been the idea of taking a revenge upon his mistress George Sand who had left him in Venice in 1834, because she simply could not endure his hysterical behaviour any more. We entirely disagree with Perceau's opinion (as published in *L'Enfer de la Bibliothèque Nationale*, 1919) which was mainly based on the preface of the 1871 edition, published by the Belgian charlatan editor Vital-Puissant, in which it was pretended that "G. Sand a collaboré avec Musset à la rédaction de ce roman de haut goût", since no arguments whatsoever are brought forward to sustain this opinion, either by Vital himself or by Perceau. To us, therefore, in company with the well known bibliographers Brunet, Gay and Bloch, de Musset has been the author. Out of revenge, out of vainness? Nobody will know, though we do find a remarkable note in this respect in the *Chassepot* (London 1868), in which we read that de Musset was the author, and Sand one of the actresses. So perhaps, after all, it was the revenge of an (often) impotent absinthe-drinker on a (at least) bisexual woman.

From *Gamiani* here follows a fragment that gives an impression of the way the lesbian theme is handled in books of this kind.

Fanny:
"What are you going to do?! Do you want to force me? Are you going to violate me again? O, no, madame! Not this time. You're going to leave me or else I'll cry for help!"

Gamiani:
"My child, we are alone! The doors are locked and I've thrown the keys out of the window. You're mine. . . ! But please, be calm . . . You need not to be afraid."

Fanny:
"My God! Don't you touch me!"

Gamiani:
"All your resistance is in vain, Fanny. You'll always give way to me. I'm much stronger than you are and my passion gives me force. No man would be able to conquer me! Look! She trembles . . . She pales! . . . My God! Fanny! My Fanny! . . . She isn't well . . . Oh, what have I done? Quiet, my dear! Quiet! When I press you against me as I do now, it is because I love you so much . . . I love you so, you, my life, my soul! Don't you understand me? Oh, I'm not bad, my little one, my love . . . No, I'm good, I'm good because I love! Look into my eyes, feel how my heart beats. It beats for you, for you alone! All I want is to please you . . . I want your intoxication in my arms. Come to yourself, my dear . . . Come to yourself under my kisses! Oh, how do I love this child! . . ."

Fanny:
"You are going to kill me! Leave me alone! My God! Leave me alone! You're horrible!"

Gamiani:

"Horrible! Horrible! What is it then that horrifies you? Am I not young like you? Am I not beautiful? Everybody says I am. And my heart! Is there another that is as capable to love as mine? The fire, that consumes me and devours me; that fire that doubles my senses and that lets me triumph where others are defeated—do you call that horrible! Tell me . . . what is a man, a lover, compared to me? He makes three or four movements; at the fourth he gasps helplessly, his body yielding in a spasm of pleasure. It's pathetic! I, on the contrary, stay strong, quivering, unsatisfied! Oh, yes! I personify the glowing pleasures of the substance, the flaming pleasures of the flesh! Luxuriously and relentlessly I give pleasure without end . . . I am the love that kills!"

Fanny:

"Enough! Gamiani! Enough!"

Gamiani:

"No! No! Listen, Fanny, listen . . . Being naked, feeling oneself young and beautiful, sweet and perfumed, burning of love and trembling of pleasure . . . touching, blending, inhaling body and soul in one breath, in one cry of love! Oh, Fanny, my Fanny, that is heaven!"

Fanny:

"What words! What glances! . . . And I listen to you, I look at you . . . Oh, pity me that I'm that weak. You fascinate me . . . What mysterious power do you have? You penetrate my flesh . . . you penetrate my bones, you're poison to me . . . Oh! Yes, you are horrible and yet . . . I love you! . . ."

Gamiani:

"I love you! I love you! Say it again and again, those are the words that burn!"

63

Gamiani was pale and motionless. Her eyes closed, her hands folded, she knelt in front of Fanny. It looked as if heaven suddenly had turned her into a marble statue. She was sublime in her annihilation and ecstasy.

Fanny:
"Yes! Yes! I love you with all the power that is in my body! I want you! I desire you! Oh, I've lost my senses!"

Gamiani:
"What do you say, my beloved? What do you say? . . . I'm happy! . . . Your hair is beautiful . . . How soft it is! It slips through my fingers, fine and gilded like silk. Your brow is pure and more white than a lily. Your eyes are beautiful, your mouth is wonderful. You are white, shiny, perfumed and heavenly from head to toes! You're an angel, you're my delight! Oh! Those roses! This lace! Be naked! . . . Come to me! . . . I'm naked already! . . . Good! That's better . . . You dazzle me! . . . Stay there, I want to admire you first. Oh! If only I could paint you! . . . Now I'm going to kiss your feet, your knees, your bosom, your mouth! Hug me! Squeeze me! More! More! What happiness! What ecstasy! She loves me!"

The two bodies seemed to melt into one. Only the heads were apart and looked at each other with a ravishing expression. The eyes were on fire, the cheeks flamingly red. The mouths quivered, smiled or passionately pressed against each other. I heard a sigh, another one answered. After that a cry, a smothered cry, and then the two women were still.

Fanny:
"I've been happy! I've been very happy!"

Gamiani:
"So was I, dear Fanny . . . I felt a happiness I've never known. Both soul and senses were on your lips . . . Come to

64

your bed . . . Let's turn this night into one of intoxication and rapture! "

After these words they both went to the alcove. Fanny rushed to the bed, stretched herself on it and laid down voluptuously. Gamiani knelt on the carpet and put her face on the girl's breast and embraced her.

Silently she looked at her . . . Very soon the caresses began again. Kisses were taken and given. Hands roamed and knew exactly where to touch . . . Fanny's eyes expressed desire and expectation; Gamiani's only a disorder of the senses. The fire of their passions whipped them up, made them blush and perspire and both of them seemed to glitter and sparkle before my eyes. Two frenzied furies indulging in rage and passion, yet putting poetically into words the excess of their debauchery: speaking in turn to the senses and the imagination.

Though I tried to reason with myself and condemned these absurd follies, I was soon excited, heated and possessed by desire. The impossible situation in which I found myself reminded me of a wild animal who devours with his eyes the female through the bars of his cage. It was impossible to join these two naked women. I had to stay silent and motionless, my head pressed against the peephole through which I, in a manner of speaking, sucked up my torment, a true torment for the damned; terrible, unbearable, beating first the head, afterwards mingling with the blood, penetrating the bones till it reached the marrow which it set on fire. I suffered more than I ever did before. It seemed to me as if my nerves, tightened and irritated, snapped. My clenched hands hit the floor. I wasn't only perspiring, I foamed at the mouth . . . Suddenly I recovered and felt irritated. My eyelids were heavy, I could hardly keep my head up. I wanted to tear myself away from my place, but then a sigh Fanny heaved made me stop . . . I injured my eyes while gazing at the scene, that jumped at me in such a horrible disorder . . .

Exhausted, Fanny let her head fall back. Gamiani rolled

over, bit the bed-sheets, chewed her hair that hung down her face. I followed their outbursts and their sighs. Like them I had reached the summit of voluptuousness!

Fanny:
"How tired I am! I feel broken, but what pleasures have I tasted!"

Gamiani:
"When the strain is lengthened, it is more painful, but the pleasure is more vivid and prolonged."

Fanny:
"So I felt. More than five minutes I was plunged into an intoxicating giddiness . . . I felt the sensation in all my limbs . . . I rolled down in the fire, in the pleasures of the senses! O madness! O happiness! Enjoyment! Now I know the meaning of that word! One thing surprises me, Gamiani . . . How is it possible that you, while still being so young, know these experiences? Where have you learned all these things? What's the origin of your passion, that overwhelmed me and sometimes frightened me?'

Gamiani:
"Ah! So you want to know me? Good! Embrace me, let's intertwine our legs and let me press you against my breast! I'm going to tell you about my life in a nunnery. It's a tale that will set our passions afire."

Fanny:
"I listen, Gamiani."

Here we leave our lesbian lovers. It will be clear, that *Gamiani*, though a classic of pornographic literature, is no ordinary "filth". It is well written and sometimes the language is extremely beautiful. It is about the only celebrated erotic novel in which no four-letter words are used. The famous work *Fanny Hill*, originally published about 1749 and including homosexual scenes, also, however, cleverly avoids the use of obscene words.

NOVELS OF THE TWENTIETH CENTURY

Gamiani was written in the nineteenth century and may be called the all-time lesbian classic. In the twentieth century popular literature brought forth many books dealing with female homosexuality. In 1928 Radclyffe Hall wrote *The Well of Loneliness*, a book that became famous. It told the story of a girl named Stephen Gordon—called Stephen because her father longed for a son he wanted to give that name. Her father brings her up as if she is a boy and a very strong father-daughter relationship develops. The normal mother-daughter rapport is entirely missing.

Radclyffe Hall was accused of painting too simple a picture of lesbianism. Psychiatrists did not like the book because the author did not give any hope to homosexual women who read it.

After an attack on *The Well of Loneliness* by the *Sunday Express* in 1928 the publishers in London were asked to show cause why the book should not be destroyed, and there was a court hearing. The magistrate said: "I have no hesitation in saying it is an obscene libel. . . . The publication of this book is an offence against public decency, an obscene libel, and I shall order it to be destroyed." In the appeal, the Attorney-General, prosecuting, said that: "The general criticism of the book is that it is missionary work, appealing for recognition of the status of people who engaged in these practices, and there is no word from start to finish to suggest that people who do these are a pest to society and their own sex."

Twenty-five years later the book was re-issued by another publisher in London without any action being taken by the authorities. It had been on sale in the United States all the time and at one juncture was selling a hundred thousand copies a year there. A biography of the masculine-styled novelist, known as "John" to her intimate friend Una, Lady Troubridge, was written by the latter under the title *The Life and Death of Radclyffe Hall*, in 1961.

About ten years after the original publication of *The Well of Loneliness*, Diana Frederics broke into print with her book *Diana*, an autobiography of a lesbian. In 1953 *Wind Woman* by Carol Hales was published. In the years that followed there came a boom in lesbian literature, especially in the United States. Donald Webster Cory in his valuable study *The Lesbian in America* was among the first who noticed this remarkable outpouring of popular literature and this is what he had to say about it in his book:

"Soft covers and bound with glue, printed on cheap paper and usually issued by obscure publishing firms, these works are seen prominently displayed in almost every drugstore and candy store where there is a paperback book-rack. It is never difficult to recognise—what the titles do not suggest, the cover photos make explicit: Splashy illusrations of a beautiful, young, half dressed lady, sprawled out voluptuously and arousingly on a bed or sofa while there is a pained but nonetheless seductive expression on her face. Behind her, there is a slightly less beautiful, somewhat older-looking woman (the age-differential stereotype is already starting to unfold) whose hair is of a different colour, and who is staring longingly at the none-too-innocent youth. She is sometimes clad in a pair of slacks and a half-buttoned shirt. Or she may be in a slip, or perhaps a neg-ligée. The scene is about to unfold: for the explosive embrace, please pay 75 cents."

Titles of these novels filled with "instant lesbianism"? Here we go: *The Pleasures We Know* ("Hell has no fury like a Lesbian scorned—and Heaven no raptures like these . . ."), *Made in Hell* ("Behind their placid, conventional marriages were two hearts crying for another kind of love"), *She Devil* ("The student taught her teacher the forbidden secrets of lust and savage cruelty"). They were written by different authors—all women by the way; that is to say, the author's name on the cover is a woman's name—but all in the same style. Reading these books one gets the impression that all these authors are in reality only a big computer, turning out lesbian novels by the dozen.

The blurb on the cover of *She Devil* is typical for this kind of novel:

"ABC's of Depravity. Vicky was the pupil—young, talented, eager to learn. Julia was the teacher—mature, experienced, and dedicated to passing her knowledge on to a rising generation. That was the way it *should* have been. In actuality, Vicky was a nubile witch on sex-greased wheels . . . and Julia had a lot to learn about the elementary facts of ecstasy and pain. The kind of ecstasy and pain that Vicky could supply with depraved delight. Once Vicky decided she wanted Julia for her willing love-slave, there was no turning back from the path of tortuous degradation . . . but no-one could predict the ultimate, twisted evil to which that path would lead! "

For those who want to know: the "ultimate, twisted evil" is that Vicky almost shies away Julia's lover whom Julia marries at the end of the book. Of course there are some variations on the theme of lesbianism. These are titles of paperbacks on a special slant of lesbianism: *World without Men* ("She stripped for men to torture them. Only other women fully enjoyed her body"), *Cloak of Evil* ("Men were her willing tormented slaves—but for love, she turned to other women"), *Off-Limits World* ("Their world is off-limits to 'normal' people. But once in a while, an innocent stranger walks into the sticky web and is trapped . . ."). And this must be the lesbian novel to end all lesbian novels: *Speak it in Whispers* ("They were mother and daughter but uncontrollable passion swept them into feverishly evil embraces").

One wonders, after having read a number of these almost but not quite pornographic novels, if an honest erotic classic like *Gamiani* that has to be sold under the counter is not much more sound than these paperbacks with their commercial stories obsessed by sex.

Strange as it seems real lesbians are not interested in novels of this kind. I have never met or heard of one who read them and for most of them these books on "the off-beat love they choose", as one of the novels calls it, is just one big laugh.

"Really," Toni said. "I'm too busy finding new partners to find the time to read trash like that!" Toni is a young, physically healthy lesbian of twenty-nine years who works as a nurse in a nursing-home. She works all day and on her evenings off she frequents one or two bars where, as she knows, lesbians are always to be found. Toni is no one-girl woman. She likes to change her partners at an astonishing rate and is not interested in a real lasting relationship.

"I just want to know their names," she once said to me. "And I don't want the same face next to me in bed more than one night . . . In that way there is no responsibility, no parting with tears in your eyes and no quarrel at the end."

It sounded very sensible, but of course Toni could not live up to her own words. She got more and more lonely. The one-night stands did not give her satisfaction any more and she turned into a neurotic. Then one day she came to ask me for advice. We had a talk and after that first visit she came back, many, many times. I cannot say that Toni has turned into a normal, heterosexual woman. Nevertheless she is much happier now, living together with a friend, a lesbian who is a few years older, and has accepted her anomaly.

During one of our talks I produced a German novel with a lesbian theme and asked Toni if she had read it.

She shook her head and said she had not.

"You know who would like to read it? The old men I'm nursing! I think these books are only written with lonely old men in mind. They must be read by men exclusively. No honest lesbian would touch them with a ten-foot pole! "

I asked Toni to forget her objections and to read the book.

"Just let me hear what you think of it," I asked her.

A week later she returned me the paperback.

"Trash," she said. "My friend read it too. Said the very same thing."

"Why?" I asked.

"You really want to know?" She smiled. "I thought you knew the answer. You're the doctor."

"Never mind that. Let me hear your opinion."

"Well . . ." She shrugged. "You know the characters in this book are not real women, let alone real lesbians! They are just dummies . . . I don't know how to put it. . . . They act strangely . . . as if sex is the only thing that matters in life . . ."

"There are women who think so . . ."

"I know . . ." She smiled again. "I think once I was one of them, but believe me, those women are different from the dummies in that stupid book. Who is the author?" She looked at the cover. "A woman. My foot. Probably it's written by a man who was hard up and needed some money . . . I bet he never met a lesbian in his whole life! "

"Your friend, does she think the same?"

"Ellen has exactly the same opinion." She turned over a few leaves. "We really got a big laugh out of it . . . We read aloud fragments . . ." She stared at me. "Why are these books never written by real lesbians? They could give a much better picture of what it means to be a lesbian . . . They could write about the pleasures it gives you and the agony . . . Only a real lesbian could explain to the public what we think and feel . . . Some day someone has to write that book."

"You could do it," I said seriously.

She shook her head.

"No, Doctor. I don't think I could . . . Maybe some day

71

when I'm older and my life is much more quiet . . . Maybe never . . ."

Toni has never written that book, but I still believe she could do it. Only a girl like Toni could write a real-life novel about her kind. Only a real lesbian could write the truth about a life of which the blurb on the cover of *The Pleasures We Know* tells us: "For in the lands ruled by Lesbos—those strange, misty islands whose inhabitants try to pass unnoticed among 'normal' people—emotions are violent and turbulent . . . and vengeance takes warped, horrifying forms! "

NOTES

1. The last two are sequels to the first. This author had a tremendous production. However, most of his pornography deals with flagellation and nates-fetishism. Almost all his books were translated into English and German, the most famous of them all being *The Memoirs of a Russian Ballet-Girl*.

2. Till the end of his life Droz denied he had written the book and even sued the publisher. The book contains a correspondence between two girls. One of them is living in the country and having affairs with men. The other is living in a boarding-school for girls and having lesbian relationships.

CHAPTER FIVE

A Lesbian Confesses

The earlier chapters of this book have been a necessary preliminary to the study of lesbianism in practice today.

As I mentioned in the Introduction, the problems of a lesbian were first brought fully home to me by a patient, whom I shall call Irmgard Lehmann, though that, of course, is not her real name. She consulted me because she was nervous, unhappy at work, suffering from insomnia and depression. During her visits to me I asked her, at one stage, and as part of the study of her case, to put down in writing her background and her problems. The following is what she wrote.

    •   •   •   •

I am Irmgard Lehmann, thirty years old. I was born in Posen and have lived there all my life. My father was a minor civil servant and my mother a school teacher. They had five children: I was the third. We were a happy family —anyhow, so it looked to outsiders.

I have always been proud of my name: even as a small child I was well aware of the circumstance that it gave me a strength I didn't possess by myself. Naturally this feeling grew less strong after I grew up but it still pleases me to introduce myself. I like to say clearly and composedly:

"I am Irmgard Wendelmuth Lehmann. How do you do?"

It startles people to hear such a formal name, formally

spoken, and more often than not they look at me with more interest than if I had mumbled:

"I'm Anna Schmidt. Pleas'd t'meet you."

I think the reason is that I always wanted to underline the fact that I exist. While I am lesbian and do not take special care to hide this fact, I have always to defend the fact that *I am*.

Something has been different since my earliest youth, even without my knowing it. I think it started in the home of my parents: my sweet dreamer of a father being gently bossed by my alert, sensible practical mother, who really was the man in the house, without having to wear the pants too overtly. My mother was one of the most female females I have ever met, and that is an amazing statement from someone who has seen her always take the lead, keep the family together, and manage the necessary money for housekeeping, education and clothing. Without my mother I doubt if my father could have ever succeeded in maintaining our standard of living.

I did not like having sisters. I would have preferred brothers—but then, I would have loved being an only child. I was in constant need of attention and love and being awkward, restrained, frustrated and showing off during the first fifteen years of my life, nobody was inclined to give me much attention and love. Even my mother didn't bother too much about me—and why should she? She had four lovely, obedient and industrious daughters to be proud of, and she was much too busy managing her job and family affairs to be able to cope with a short, not so attractive adolescent that happened to be her daughter too. As far as I can remember, I felt myself an outsider. One who does not belong.

My sisters had their boy-friends; they fell in and out of love with normal regularity. One way or another I couldn't be interested in that everlasting subject of long, intense discussions between my four sisters: love. Sometimes I listened to their opinions on boys they knew and after

74

having listened I was always wondering what on earth they saw in them. I was then about sixteen years old and I didn't know what it meant to be in love.

At that time I left school and went to work in a bookshop. My mother had chosen this position; she had heard of the vacancy and said:

"Irmgard, you like to read so you'll probably like to sell books. You go to that bookshop and apply for the job."

I went to the bookshop, applied for the job and got it.

I stayed there for two years and did not only learn to hate selling books but also how to make love. The manager was a friendly middle-aged man who left it to his second-in-command to coach and instruct me.

Coach and instruct me she did—and not only as far as selling books was concerned. I loved her, and she fascinated me and made me realise that women appealed to me much more than men. Now I understood why I was never interested in the love affairs of my sisters; if I had had brothers I might have discovered the truth about myself much sooner. As it was I needed Lise to get to know all about myself.

I started my first job on the third of October, one day before autumn took possession of the streets good and proper. I liked going out in a gale and walking through heavy rain, even if it meant my getting soaked through. At the end of the first week I kept some dry clothes in the little ladies'-room at the back of the shop, went from home dressed in slacks, mackintosh and galoshes, and changed into something more suitable after I reached the shop.

One morning I arrived soaked through and went to the ladies'-room to change. I took off my coat, removed my jersey and my slacks in order to dress myself in a simple black frock that my mother had given me, considering it the right wear for a salesgirl in a bookshop. I was standing in my slip when the door was opened and Lise Hofer came in. Lise, who was then still "Miss Hofer" to me, was a handsome woman, about thirty years old, dark,

75

strong and dominant. From the very first day I had been a little bit afraid of her, though she never gave reason for fear. She was kind in a offhand manner, very competent and as far as I in my limited experience could make out, the best saleswoman in the town.

As she came in I looked up startled and crossed my arms over my breasts; my hands covered my bare shoulders. She looked at me and suddenly I felt as if I were stark naked, instead of being quite decently dressed in a neat, black slip.

"Oh . . . I'm . . . I'm sorry," I stammered. "I didn't know you'd come in."

"Never mind," she said. "You look lovely, dear. What a nice figure you have! "

She crossed the room and stood right in front of me. There was something in her eyes—a question, some sort of an appeal—that made me blush and feel terribly unsure of myself. Suddenly she put out her hand, stroked my cheek and let her fingertips very lightly touch my throat.

"How lovely you are," she said. "So young. So—clean."

I'll never forget that she said just that: so clean. Later I learned that Lise had a passion for cleanliness; not a passion that made her a kind of soap-and-water addict, but a distinct and quite normal preference for orderliness. She liked herself and everything she possessed neat and clean; I have never seen her with a button off or a run in her nylons and she hated people that didn't wash themselves properly or that didn't look after their clothes as they ought to.

I looked up at her and suddenly I saw the admiration in her eyes—admiration mingled with a kind of burning intensity that I could not yet place or understand. I shivered and she put her arms around me.

"Poor baby," she said softly. "You are cold."

I rested against her; I felt her strong body, her firm breasts, unexpectedly soft and warm, her hands on my bare back. And then I felt a strange, strong emotion, exploding

76

in the depths of my body, possessing me, enveloping me in an overwhelming desire to surrender to this tender and trusting embrace. I lifted my face and looked at her; in my eyes she must have seen what I felt, for she gazed at me with a new, knowing look, full of a triumphant gratitude. And then she bent her head and kissed me quickly, warmly, on my lips—it was a little bit of a kiss, but it staggered me, it threw me over, it put me forever in her arms: I was in love for the first time.

Not more than five seconds passed but that was enough for me to know myself, to know Lise—to know the whole situation between us without understanding it.

Immediately after she kissed me Lise let me go and turned around. She stood at the window and looked at the desolate yard behind the shop. She didn't say a word.

I didn't speak either. I took my black frock out of the cupboard and put it on. Then I stood in front of the mirror and combed my hair. When I looked at my face I had a shock: my eyes were brilliant, my cheeks a rosy red and my lips glowed. Suddenly I thought myself quite pretty and that too was the first time.

Behind me Lise moved. I saw her face appear in the mirror; she looked at me and I looked at her—our looks crossed in the no-man's-land between our images and ourselves. I wanted to say something but I didn't dare to speak. I didn't trust my voice. I waited and after a while Lise said:

"We must talk, Irmgard, darling. Can I see you tonight?"

I wanted to call out: yes, yes, you can see me tonight; you can see me every night, if you want to! But instead I listened wonderingly to a new voice, deep inside me, that told me exactly what to do and after a short hesitation I said:

"I'm sorry, Miss Hofer. I'm busy tonight."

"Tomorrow then?"

"I don't know yet. I'll let you know."

One more moment Lise looked at me and I knew she understood. It wasn't me that told her to wait; it was the voice of my new power over her and it was right that I listened to what it said.

That day I walked and worked as if in a dream, and after I came home I told my mother that Miss Hofer wanted me to come over to her flat to talk about books and bookselling. My mother smiled and said:

"That's nice, dear. You must be doing well, otherwise she wouldn't have shown such an interest in you."

Sometime during the next day I told Miss Hofer I could make it and that I would be at her flat at seven-thirty.

She didn't ask me to have dinner with her and I think she knew I would have said "no" if she had asked me. The house was large and sombre and rather forbidding, but I forgot about that when I reached the top floor where Lise had her apartment. It was a lovely apartment: large and comfortable. I stood in the doorway and looked around the room, knowing I could be happy here. Lise pushed me gently into the room and entered it after me. She closed the door and leant against it.

"Hello, Irmgard," she said softly.

I turned around and looked at her. She had changed after she came home: she wore dark slacks and a very light grey cashmere sweater that made the deep chestnut of her hair more glowing than ever. I opened my mouth as if I wanted to speak, but I didn't make a sound. I stared at her and it seemed as if I lost myself in her eyes. I went back to her and quite naturally, quite simply she took me in her arms. Again I felt her body against mine; again the explosion of emotions took place deep within me and suddenly I was happy—gloriously, frighteningly happy for the very first time in all my sixteen sad years. I started to tremble but this time Lise didn't say that I was cold. She just held me and could feel the warmth of my body. I rested my head on her shoulder and let her hands do what they wanted to do.

78

She caressed my back, the back of my head; her fingers travelled down again—suddenly I felt her touch the bare flesh of my body. I stood so still—it was as if I didn't dare to move, afraid that she would stop loving me if I moved.

She undid my bra and I strained my breasts till her fingers found them: she caressed them softly, softly—and then, in one fierce quick movement, she bent my head backwards and kissed me hard and long.

My arms, my legs, all of me went heavy; I was afraid I would fall, but then I heard Lise's voice:

"Oh, Irmgard, darling Irmgard—Irmgard, please, forgive me! You are so sweet..."

"Why must I forgive you?" I whispered. "I like you and I like what you do to me."

I really was innocent; I didn't know what I was talking about. Lise must have understood for she stood several moments without saying anything. But then I heard her take in her breath; it was as if she pulled herself together. Her fingers sought and found my bra again, but this time she fastened it and pulled my jersey down. She put her arm around my shoulders and led me to a couch at the far end of the large room.

"Sit down," she said. "We must talk—you and I."

We talked and at that time I learned something about the position of homosexuals.

"But I wanted you to kiss me," I said. "I wanted you to put your arms around me." And then, with youthful naïvety I added: "I *made* you kiss me."

Lise laughed.

"Do you really love me?" I asked.

"Yes," she said without hesitation. "I liked you from the very first moment we met and very soon I loved you deeply."

I said wonderingly:

"Did you think about me? I mean, after you came home did you sit here and think of me?"

79

I was altogether sixteen years old and suddenly very proud to be the heroine of a very real love-affair. It didn't occur to me than that this love-affair was rather unusual and quite different from the affairs my sisters discussed so glowingly and so often. Up to that time I had been quite innocent. My mother never bothered about relating to me the facts of life. She took it for granted that I should find out for myself.

Now I know that my own mother was more inhibited than I have ever been; now I can understand and forgive her. There has been a time, when I was about twenty years old, that I hated her for not loving me as I needed to be loved; and for not protecting me as I needed to be protected.

In any case, Lise came along at just the right moment: I was ready for love; I longed for personal attention, and after all the harsh remarks my family made about me it was quite intoxicating to hear soft words of love and tenderness.

Sitting on that couch in Lise's living-room I became a lesbian—I did not know it at that time but when thinking back in later years I always arrive at that one moment when Lise simply said she loved me. She was the first one to do so in all my short life.

Lise taught me more about life than any other person ever has. When she found out how ignorant I was she set out to explain all that I had never known or understood. She started on that first night and tried very hard not to make love to me—I think she wanted to wait till I was just a little bit more self-sufficient. But now that I had felt what love can do, I wanted it to fulfil its promise. If there was ever a time that a minor seduced a grown-up it was then. After a time I stopped listening to what she told me. I moved a little and sat quite close to her, my head rested against her arm. Never before had I tried to make love. but now it was as if I had known all along what to do. Above and behind me I heard her voice, a clear well-bred

80

voice that was nice to listen to. I put my hand on her knee and let it travel upwards till it reached the soft sweater. There it hesitated, but only for a moment—deep within me I felt a terrible longing, a feverish thrill that made me go on. My fingers crept higher and at last touched her breast. I heard the sharp intake of breath as she felt the soft pressure; it was as if she waited for what I should do.

But I didn't do anything. I sat motionless, cupping my hand around her breast, not knowing what was expected of me. We stayed thus for a long, still moment and then Lise said softly:

"Oh, Irmgard . . . are you very, very sure about all this?"

"I don't know what to be sure about," I answered. "I don't know what to do."

One more moment we stayed without speaking, without moving. And then, suddenly, Lise took me in her arms and covered my face with kisses. She was quite different from the rather serious and solemn person she had been just a little while earlier. She was warm, living, very much in love and an expert in the art of showing it.

I don't know how I got undressed but suddenly I found myself lying on the couch with Lise softly caressing my young, slim body.

Have I ever been happier than at that moment, when I discovered I had a body and what it could do to me? So virginal, so really childish was I that up till that moment I had never known the wild feelings of life itself. It was as if I were born all over again—but this time a soft and terrible birth, a gentle and fiery welcome into a world I didn't know existed.

Lise's hands were so sweet on my breasts, on my arms, my legs. They stroked my loins and after that caressed me so tenderly that my arching body trembled under the touch of her fingers.

81

She kissed me—again and again, finding out what I liked best and all the time waiting a half-second for my reaction.

Thinking back I know that during those first hours I was most definitely formed into the lesbian I am now—later I made love with a man, but never once did I find this unending patience Lise showed. Always the man I was in bed with seemed so eager to get what he wanted, so impatient to reach the ultimate goal, that all his ministrations seemed kind of hasty and not really meant to love me and the body I live in.

Is it this patience that appeals to me or is it simply a disposition I am born with? I don't know. Nobody knows. Nobody has ever found out why people are homosexuals. I have thought about this; again and again I have tried to find reasons for being what I am but I always fail. And now I have given up thinking about it—I take myself the way I am. I'm not glad to be a homosexual; many of my homosexual friends claim to be very satisfied with their lot, but I often think that a way of defending oneself which is rather pathetic. Homosexuals do not lead an easier life than other people; on the contrary, our life is harder and much more demanding than that of the doting husband and loving wife. We miss all the advantages of ordinary married or normal bachelor life. But still, I, for my part, am grateful to have experienced moments of real happiness—like that first moment with Lise, when we found each other at last in a close embrace, and in which I reached for the first time in my life my point of no return.

Lise and I were together for two years, during which we loved each other deeply and honestly. The strange thing is that our bodily love was important to us but by no means as important as the love that made Lise teach me the art of living decently and honestly and that made me accept her as the one person I could always ask for advice. She was not my mother—there has been a time that I thought Lise a substitute for the mother I needed and never got—

but she was not that. Even with the difference in age between us we were equals—she respected me as much as I respected her.

It was Lise who taught me to become a strong, clean human being, both in mind and in body—I still remember very clearly what she told me during those two happy years in which I had to deceive my parents constantly but in which too I lived more uprightly and more consciously than ever before. I am not sorry to have deceived my parents—I had no other choice. Had they been more realistic and recognised me for what I am, they could have helped me in the process of growing up, but that was not the case. They had their image of a daughter and I had to stick to that instead of the other way round. It was Lise who made me love them with a rather tolerant but very real love that made me understand them as they ought to have understood me.

I think I would have been very happy with Lise for years to come if she had not died. But she did die—a very ordinary, run-of-the-mill death that made no more than two or three lines in the papers. She was struck by a car, taken to hospital and that was all there was to it.

The next morning I went to the shop as always, thinking of the night ahead. Lise and I saw each other four nights a week; my mother was very proud of the attention Lise gave me and told me over and over again how grateful I ought to be for all those concerts, plays and ballet-performances that Lise and I attended.

The manager was standing in the middle of the shop and when I came in he looked at me with a forlorn, helpless look and said:

"Oh, Irmgard, what must we do?"

Quickly I asked:

"What is the matter? What has happened? Is something wrong? Where is Miss Lise?"

I looked around me and didn't see his face when he said:

83

"Lise is dead, Irmgard."

Twelve years ago he said those words but when I think of them this moment, I still hear them very clearly as if someone quite near me speaks.

On that morning I left the shop and walked the streets, went to the flat, but couldn't get in, and then went home. My mother was there, busily arranging household matters, talking with the baker and later with my father and later again with my sisters.

"Irmgard does not feel well," she said. "Miss Hofer has had a street accident and has died."

They tried to help me and cheer me up but I wouldn't let them. I don't know what strange form of masochism possessed me, but one of the first things I did was to go along with my sisters to the dance-hall where they spent their Saturday nights. You may call it escapism. I did not want to face the fact that I had only now begun to live and had just lost everything that made life worth while.

Two weeks after Lise was buried I walked out with a young man named Richard; three months after that we got engaged and less than a year later I married him. When I think back to that time I hate myself. It has been the darkest period in my life till now; I was not more than a egocentric, egotistic child, that wanted to be made a fuss of. Now I think that Lise's death taught me even more than all she had said to me.

I hated Richard and all that he stood for from the very first moment he kissed me. He was a nice enough boy, but his hot, hasty hands on my body made me sick. Still, I let him for I had made up my mind to marry. As a married woman I would get away from my mother who had started to nag me since I went to the dance-hall with my sisters. Suddenly she had discovered another daughter —one she hadn't noticed so much up till now, but who promised to be quite beautiful. I had been an ugly child, a rather dowdy girl, but suddenly I became transformed into a very attractive young woman with blue eyes and

84

black hair, a slim, straight body and a soft, gentle voice. I knew I would never have a chance if I did not get away from home, and silently pleading Lise's forgiveness I made Richard love me, knowing that I could never love him.

During our engagement he tried to make love to me, but I always put him off by telling him that I would have none of that till we were married. That's why we married so soon afterwards: Richard was twenty-seven, had a good job as an engineer and being a quiet, sensible young man, had some money saved.

I was the first one to be married; my mother was very moved and cried a lot during the ceremony, my sisters were green with envy, my father was grave and couldn't care less.

I left my home and went to live with Richard in the rooms that we had prepared in the weeks before our marriage. It was near the house where Lise and I had been so happy. I thought of that when Richard carried me over the threshold, telling me that he would have preferred a proper honeymoon with all the trimmings. I was the one who didn't want a honeymoon—the only thing I wanted was to get away from home. Now I had left my home for good and here was Richard, eager, in love, all man, all husband. He had waited so long for his supreme moment that all his patience had worn out.

He took me straight to our bedroom and finally I had to give in. I closed my eyes to shut the tears out and let him fondle my bare breasts, my cold body. I let him kiss my lips and waited for him to kiss and caress the rest of me, but that never happened. Suddenly he made a funny sort of choking sound and covered me with his body. Though he was getting his satisfaction, I only felt a sharp, prolonged pain, that got worse and worse.

"Richard! Stop!" I cried out but he had forgotten all about me. He was breathing very hard, not knowing that I knew nothing about the act he was about to perform.

At last I didn't struggle any longer. I lay quite still and

let the tears slip out from under my eyelids. The pain was hot and omnipresent; I lay in a bed of pain, in the arms of a man I didn't and couldn't love.

Later, in the weeks before our divorce, Richard and I have talked often about those first married hours. By that time I had learned to respect and even love him—but that wasn't a love that could keep man and wife together. In the end I told Richard all about Lise and about myself. He came to understand my feelings and even went so far as to consult doctors and psychiatrists who assured him that I was less of a freak than the world would have made me out had it known about me.

Out of the first forceful unions of Richard and me Hildegarde was born. Nine months and ten days after our marriage she came into the world, unaware of the fact that she saved me from many difficult hours during the six or seven months before her birth. During my pregnancy I was very sick and the doctor told Richard to leave me alone.

When Hildegarde was a few months old Richard tried to renew our marital relationship and it was then that I decided I couldn't go on with it. At last Lise succeeded in what she had taught me: her honesty and her courage made me tell Richard who and what I was.

I won't talk about the very difficult months that followed; I presume that everybody can imagine the hard times we had. It was more difficult for Richard; he had to understand something that didn't belong to his world; he had to try and respect feelings he hardly knew existed. He was the prototype of an outsider: his knowledge of homosexuality came from rather sordid jokes.

I know now that I wronged Richard immensely. The way he accepted my being a lesbian has made me respect, and in a way, love him, more than I ever did during our marriage.

There is one thing for which I have longed since this episode with Richard: if only people took the trouble to try and get acquainted with homosexuality before they go and condemn it. I do not mean they have to go out and be homosexuals themselves—like priests who go to work in coal-mines to get to know the miners. An outsider can never know or understand the real homosexual; he can only know and understand homosexuality. Books are written on this subject; great minds have produced theories on it—but the people, for the greater part, do not take the trouble to read those books or to listen to those theories. They judge and condemn without knowing what they judge and condemn.

Here I was then, free again, or, better, at last free. I took a vow never again to play hide-and-seek with myself. I was a lesbian and I had to live it. I did not think it right to accept money from Richard although he was quite willing to give it. I had to earn money for myself and my daughter. But how? A job was out of the question. I had to be near Hildegarde. And further: had I not decided to be myself? Taking a job would mean that I should have to pretend to be normal. I took up writing. Little by little I succeeded in making my own independent living.

But that's not important. What matters is how did I propose to realise my earnest will to be myself? I must confess that I had only vague notions about it, at the time. The struggle to earn a living made it not difficult for me to ignore the demands of the body. Having established myself as a writer and having succeeded in finding a market for my articles that problem became more acute. I started frequenting "gay places". Nobody can stop oneself from building images. I had canonised my affair with Lise. She had become a kind of saint, and our affair holy. So I did not want to start something in the same way. The contacts that I looked for and found were purely of the flesh. The first was Helen. I met her in one of the cafés. We were sitting side by side at the bar and she started the game by offering me a drink. A conversation was begun. I felt awkward. That we finally went away together was mostly Helen's work. She was an old hand at the game. We went to my home.

87

"So this is where you live?" she said, looking curiously about her. "Quite cosy."

I pretended to be busy arranging things. Helen sat down and waited. After some time she came behind me and put her hands on my shoulders.

"Why are you so nervous?' she asked. "I'm not a man-eating tigress, you know. Let's sit down and talk."

"I was wondering," I said hesitantly, "what you must think of me," at the same time realising the stupidity of my remark.

"That you need someone," she answered, adding pensively after a short pause, "or something." She put an arm around my shoulder and drew me to her. "Come on, don't act like a shy spinster, for you don't look like one, you know. You may not be as experienced as I am, but you are no stranger at it."

Softly she kissed my cheek and stroked my hair. "How beautiful you are," she murmured in my ear. She turned my face towards her and kissed me on the mouth. I had almost forgotten how it was to be kissed on the mouth and it gave me a thrill. With lips pressed together we remained for some time, inhaling each other's breath, then she touched my lips with the tip of her tongue. Taking courage soon afterwards she slipped it into my mouth and explored it, gently pressing my tongue. It filled me with lust, I felt the blood rushing to my head and started answering her kiss. That lasted for a long time. While her right hand was busy touching my breasts I unconsciously realised that, for the second time, a human being was discovering the treasures my body had to offer, and I almost swooned for joy. Without knowing it, I was stroking her hair and massaging the nape of her neck. She took my hand away and guided it towards her own body. Helen gazed deep into my eyes. "I know that you don't love me, but you do like me, don't you?"

"Yes," I panted. I felt my lust steadily mounting. After all the years of abstinence the feeling was almost unbearable. I slipped my hand somewhat timidly and almost unwillingly under her skirts. I stopped a moment on her knees, caressing them, then let it creep slowly and stealthily up. Then I took courage and she sighed contentedly. Her arms were encircling my body, her breath was going spasmodic—I did no more thinking, just did.

"Darling," she panted, "let's undress."

Almost reluctantly I let go of her. She took my already unbuttoned blouse off. She herself was now clad only in a flimsy garment. Hurriedly I undressed myself further.

"Let me look at you, darling," she whispered, "Just let me look at you . . ."

I stood erect at her side and looked down, noticing everything: her parted pouting lips, her beautiful breasts, her tender nipples, seemed to be asking for those caresses she was so fond of; over all her body was a shivering of insatiable desire. I noticed a rippling on her belly, like wind blowing over a stretch of water, and I think it was that which made me lose control over myself. This tantalising body I had to possess at all costs, the only thing that mattered in the world. Instinct drove me to do things I never knew I could do; I behaved like a madwoman. I do not know how many times I realised desire—but at last I sank down on my knees in front of the sofa, totally exhausted. Slowly, very slowly I regained my senses. I hid my head in my hands. I was filled with shame. A hand stroked my head gently. "You must have been sexually starved, dear," the soft, now husky voice of Helen said.

"For years," I answered. "I don't know what has come over me . . . I was completely carried away by . . . by what, yes, by what? Have I hurt you? I must apologise, I could not help it . . ."

She turned on her side, resting on her elbow, facing me.

"Apologise?" she said, "dear me, you don't know what you're saying. This is what I have been longing for all my life, what I have been dreaming about, always hoped to find with every conquest I made, but never did—up till now.

This has been the most wonderful experience I ever had, the only one worth mentioning, in fact.

"Just imagine," she continued, "me supposing you an ingénue, whom I should have to teach everything . . ."

Her praise of my unconscious behaviour startled me. I did not want her to fall in love with me. As I mentioned before, I did not want to start a regular affair ever again. I do not know whether it was a question of thought-reading or whether she fostered the same fear. For I did not expect her next words.

"It was a wonderful experience, a unique happening, something that can never be repeated. Before you start wondering about my intentions, I must tell you that I am an alleycat, always on the lookout for adventures; it's the tension I need, the unexpected. A lasting relationship has never been my intention and will never be. I know that it means loneliness in the future and loneliness is the most dreaded thing among lesbians. But when I see a middle-aged lesbian couple trudging down the street I always get a stale taste in my mouth. Better end up alone."

I have given the story of Helen and me at such length because I think it reveals a lot about myself and the cause of the trouble I was consulting you about.

After Helen I have had many, many other affairs. I am a kind of lesbian nymphomaniac, I suppose. The reason for my hitherto promiscuous conduct is now quite apparent to me. It can never give lasting satisfaction, because tenderness and affection are lacking. I have been missing the affection and the tenderness. It is the main—no, only, source of my neurosis. I must get rid of the notion that my initial lesbian relationship cannot be repeated. Some day I hope to encounter a partner who can fill the vacuum left by Lise.

.   .   .   .

In psychiatry the patient has to solve his or her own problems. It is the task of the psychiatrist to explain the meaning of certain symptoms or symbols and make suggestions about the places where delvings may prove successful. For delving in the subconscious is what has to be done to find the origin of the dilemmas which cause the suffering. Generally it is not an easy enterprise, and it takes often several years before the patient obtains a clear understanding of the inhibitions that cause the distress. The success of an analysis is greatly dependent on the extent of co-operation and the intelligence of the patient. The case of Irmgard Lehmann is one of the few cases where the analysed person solved her own problem without much assistance from the psychiatrist.

CHAPTER SIX

Are Lesbians Born That Way?

Nobody ever accused the famous sexologist Magnus Hirschfeld of exaggeration. Yet he made some sensational statements and discovered a number of facts that gave the world a new, totally changed impression of some phenomena of human life and in particular of human sex-life.

In one of his books[1] Hirschfeld states that there are twice as many female as male homosexuals. He estimates the ratio of visible to camouflaged female homosexuals as one to one hundred and found that most of these camouflaged homosexual women are married and have children of their own.

These remarkable revelations turn the phenomenon of lesbianism into a problem that is getting more and more important every day. In ancient Greece the island of Lesbos gave its name to lesbianism, but the role women played in Greek society was an insignificant one. Unlike male homosexuality lesbianism was not a phenomenon of great importance in ancient Greece, though as indicated in the first chapter it was certainly well known and recorded.

How different is the situation in our days!

Now women play a very important part in modern society. They serve as soldiers, work as policewomen, civil servants and nurses, manage factories and have found their places as teachers, lawyers, journalists. Female doctors and psychiatrists benefit the welfare of mankind. The emancipation of women changed the face of the world and one of

92

the consequences was that female homosexuality came more into the open than it ever did in world history.

Modern man makes a strange distinction between male and female homosexuality. Even in countries with a tolerant legislation male homosexuality often is frowned upon and female homosexuality is accepted. Why? Is it because it is much easier to camouflage a relationship between two women than between two men? Women can kiss each other, walk arm in arm and share an apartment and not a voice will be heard against them. Two men sharing an apartment immediately raise suspicion.

Why?

It is not only the public that makes this strange distinction. Authorities do the very same thing, for instance in England. The new German penal code states that homosexual acts between men, no matter whether they are committed in public or not, are punishable by law. The question: "But what about homosexual acts between women?" is answered by the legislator in this way:

"The objections raised by those interested in saying that the law on homosexual acts committed by men is contrary to the equality of rights of men and women as stated by law, are without importance. The biological sexual distinction between man and woman gives a clear picture of the relation and turns all comparative elements into factors of no importance. Homosexual acts between women are caused by different reasons and the consequences for human society are less. It is not necessary to punish this phenomenon by law."[2]

Pauly[3] protested in 1961: "As a reason for this discrimination it is propounded that it is very difficult to distinguish commonly accepted friendly acts between women from homosexual acts. In southern countries where people are more unconcerned and temperaments livelier the same thing could easily be said about men." Laura Hutton in her book *The Single Woman* makes it clear she thinks it more advisable for unmarried women to practise lesbianism than heterosexual "fornication". Imagine the indignation if an author had given the same advice to unmarried men!

Again we ask: why this inexplicable discrimination between two phenomena that are basically the same and that have—as we shall see later on in this chapter—the same cause?

The reason for this enigmatic attitude of authorities and public is an emotional one and not as inexplicable as one might think. Though *coitus per anum* is not a *conditio sine qua non* for a homosexual relationship between two men, and as a matter of fact is less frequently practised than the public is inclined to think, fellatio (taking the penis in the mouth) and mutual masturbation most of the time are the backbone of such a relationship. All these practices between men are heavily tabooed because of the ejaculation and consequently "loss" of sperm that is the result.

It is this "loss" of sperm that makes a homosexual act between men such a deadly sin. It is this "crime" the German legislator meant when he spoke of "consequences for human society". It is a strange thing that in a century of alarming over-population our judgement is still guided by emotions dating back to Biblical times when in barren, empty and under-populated surroundings a wilful loss of semen indeed could be regarded as a "crime against society". Of course the opinion of the Church which states that every spilling of sperm that is caused by an act not regarded as normal coition is a deadly sin, plays an important part in judging the behaviour of male homosexuals.

Another important reason for discrimination is the following fact. The male sex act, whether heterosexual or homosexual, is basically an act of violence. He wants to seduce, possess, penetrate, rape the object of his lust; according to Sigmund Freud there is always a certain need to humiliate present. With unbalanced persons this may easily lead to crimes, especially when the act is committed with minors. The sex crimes we read about in the papers are a lot of the time committed by men upon minors, boys or girls. Of

94

course many homosexuals prefer young boys, but not all of them. There are as many homosexuals who prefer older men, most probably "father substitutes".

The same can be said of female homosexuals. Many of them prefer young girls. But it seldom or never leads to violation, primarily because there is no need for humiliation (though as previously mentioned, sadistic elements sometimes exist), secondly because there is much more tenderness and affection involved.

In contrast with the ideas the public has about the goings-on between homosexual men is the image in the public mind regarding lesbian relationships. Lesbianism is not associated with detested practices such as rectal intercourse and fellatio, but with innocent actions such as kissing and embracing—incorrectly as we shall see. In the public mind lesbian relationships have more emotional than physical aspects and therefore are more "pure".

It was the French author Paul Reboux[4] who observed: "In regard to men who are feminine, public opinion is ruthless. Dignified old gentlemen make no secret of their indignation. No doubt they had one or two very intimate male friends in their youth. So what? Disgusted and with stern faces they condemn these actions. How different their attitude as soon as they are dealing with women who are men! They wink elatedly. Enthusiasm fills their eyes when they observe two women who are lost in a passionate embrace. Yet they are the very same people that would howl with indignation when they saw two men act in the same way. Their attitude is guided by the ancient theory regarding human secretion. Not a drop of it is to be lost. And as long as there are women involved, not a drop of this precious substance is going to be lost . . ."

There is still another reason why the public refuses to take lesbian relationships seriously. Noël Coward hinted about it when, in one of his books[5] a girl observes with regard to a lesbian relationship of two other girls: "I think it must be very boring if one doesn't have something to put into something." Frank S. Caprio[6] states in the words of a psychiatrist: "It is my opinion that a very important unconscious factor in the distinction between the legal treatment of male and female homosexuals lies in the fact that the male ego does not wish to recognise that women could possibly secure sexual satisfaction without the participation of the opposite sex. The tendency for judges not to prosecute female homosexuals, perhaps, is an unconscious expression of denying its existence. Psychoanalysts use this mechanism of denying that which they do not wish to accept as a fact as 'Psychic Annulment'."

Most homosexual relationships between men and lesbian relationships between women are fruits of the same tree. That tree is called: the Oedipus Complex.

A LESBIAN IS MADE

Though in a very few cases men and women are "born homosexuals", most of the time homosexuality is acquired in infancy as a consequence of a disturbance in development. The absence of partners of the other sex can cause a homosexual period during puberty in the same way that homosexual acts are practised in prison, or at sea, for instance, by heterosexual men and women who are in need of partners. As soon as partners of the other sex are available, these homosexual tendencies disappear for the greater part.

Of course there are women who had sexual relations with other girls when they were still children and who knew then already what their taste was going to be. But that is not the hard and fast rule. The six lesbians interviewed by the editors of *Dialoog* were asked when they felt attracted to women for the first time in their life. Only two admitted having felt this attraction when they were still children (twelve and fourteen). One confessed she was thirty-three

TWO GIRLS
From the painting by Jules Pascin

THE LOVERS
From the painting by Jules-Robert Auguste
(The Louvre)

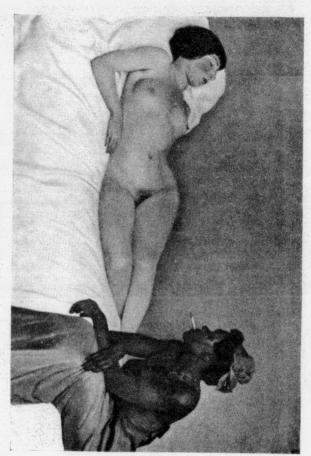

THE WHITE AND THE BLACK
From the painting by Felix Vallotton
(Hahnloser Collection, Winterthur)

ETERNITY
From the painting by Leonor Fini

and had a husband and two children when she felt attracted to another woman for the first time. Another was twenty-five and engaged to be married, when she (a youth-leader) was seduced by the mother of a boy. One of the interviewed lesbians was married and had three children, before she, at the age of forty-three, fell in love with another woman. Of the unmarried women who were interviewed one was twenty eight when she discovered the truth about herself.

Homosexual men who are hostile towards women always make an exception for their mother, in the same way as lesbians who hate men make an exception for their father. This is caused by the fact that male homosexuality arises from a very intimate connection with the mother and a very strained relation with the father. As a consequence woman becomes a tabooed subject and the man who has to give up the mother as a love-subject, identifies with her and takes over her part. The same goes for a girl who becomes a lesbian. The intimacy the girl feels when with her father, the rivalry of her mother and the giving up of the father as a subject for sexual relations, causes her to identify with him and to take over his part.

In the case of a girl the development is more complicated, as in infancy her first experience of love is through her mother. Though the starting-point of the development is the same, the outcome is different. As Edmund Bergler[7] states:

"The striking feature in Lesbians' development is that they cannot, as can the male homosexual, flee to 'another continent'—man. Lesbians remain with the first object of fear, without the flight to Ultima Thule. How is this possible and how do they manage?

"When a child has a masochistic attachment, and is incapable of shifting this terrifying attachment, either partially or in its entirety, on other persons, one result is certain: the inner torture machine starts its barrage of reproaches. What follows, inevitably, is installation of an inner alibi, a 'defence mechanism'. (. . .) The inner layer

97

(the unconscious ego) always works on the 'itinerary of the opposite': if the individual is accused of forbidden pleasure (libido), the inner layer mobilises derivatives of the opposite: hatred. Thus the child 'hates' her mother as an inner alibi. Since one cannot live in peace with the inner torturer for any length of time, the *pseudo*hatred (for neurotics are capable only of ersatz emotions, of pseudo-aggression!) is in its turn vetoed, and the itinerary of the opposites is again invoked to provide the next alibi—the alibi of *pseudo*love. This alibi leads straight to Lesbianism.

"Viewed through the analytic microscope, Lesbianism is shown to be composed of five layers: Layer 1: Masochistic attachment to mother; Layer 2: Veto of inner conscience, forbidding 'pleasure in displeasure'; Layer 3: First defense of pseudohatred; Layer 4: Second reproach of inner conscience, vetoing hatred of any kind for the mother; Layer 5: Second defense of pseudolove.

"Thus Lesbianism is not 'woman's love for woman', but the pseudolove of a masochistic woman, admitting to an inner alibi that she consciously does not understand. The irony is unsurpassed."

Bergler's theories are not completely in agreement with our first theory of the development of the Oedipus Complex in lesbians—a proof of the discord on this subject which is found in the world of science. New theories keep supplanting old ones and the result is an ever-changing opinion on the why's and how's of lesbianism.

Though the last word about the cause of female homosexuality is not yet spoken, there are some facts one has to know if one wishes to cope with the problem successfully. Some of the undermentioned misgivings about lesbianism have had a very long life, but only if we know them to be just myths can we paint a proper likeness of lesbianism in the following chapters. First of all we have to do away with superstitions and popular beliefs such as:

(a) Lesbians abhor men and are not capable of enjoying sexual relations with them

Here we have another one of those "black-and-white statements". Of course there are some lesbians who do not want to have anything to do with men, one way or the other. But their number is comparatively small; they are not representative of lesbians as a whole. The masculine type of lesbian generally likes to mix up with men, as a man among men. The feminine type of lesbian generally avoids too friendly contacts with men, anticipating implications she does not want: but not because she dislikes men. As always, the truth lies in the middle.

Dialoog[9], a Dutch bi-monthly "for homosexuality and society" dedicated a whole issue to lesbianism. A number of lesbians were interviewed. One of them remarked: "What I think of men depends entirely on their personality. Some I like, others I don't. I love to flirt with the ones I like." Another said: "I think men are easier to live with than women." Only one of them declared: "To me they all look alike. They look like Chinese to me. In my relations with them I'm not very tolerant. I have more patience with women. Why, I don't know." Out of six lesbians two were married and had children. Psychiatrists dealing regularly with lesbians found many of them actually enjoyed sexual relations with men and had coital orgasm.

As for the large group of bisexual women and facultative lesbians (those who can enjoy sexual intercourse with women, but can very well do without), they have no troubles at all in their contacts with men.

Outsiders, ill at ease with phenomena they cannot explain from their own experience, are often apt to jump to easy conclusions.

(b) Once a woman has been made love to by a lesbian, she is lost for men

The outsider's reasoning is, "a woman knows much

better than a man where the sensitive places are, she knows best what a woman will like. Then too there is no danger of pregnancy. Also a woman has no cares about an erection and a ejaculatio praecox. She can go on infinitely till her partner has reached an orgasm. These reasonings are all very true. Only—a woman who is not a lesbian, either consciously or unconsciously, will always go back to the opposite sex, regardless of the risk of getting in the family way (there may even be a strong undercurrent to seek the risk of pregnancy) and in spite of all the above-mentioned advantages.

(c) Many a woman becomes a lesbian through excessive self-abuse

Some persons reason that a woman who has indulged in too much masturbation cannot be brought to an orgasm by a man. Hence her turning to women to seek satisfaction. They forget the fact that another human being can cause much greater tension and excitement than one's own hand, or any lifeless corpus alieni can do. Not to forget the mysterious influence of "love". If a woman is heterosexual by nature, that other person will be a man.

Since Kinsey shook the world with his statistics, we know that practically everybody, male or female, has indulged in masturbation for a longer or shorter period. We have no longer to fear for and believe in "after-effects".

(d) It is easy to detect a lesbian

The starting-point is that some masculine lesbians like to dress in a manly fashion; actually, many a purely heterosexual woman does the same. As for resoluteness and boldness—especially in the lower regions of society we find many resolute and bold women who are not lesbians.

The feminine lesbian usually dresses herself very well and in a very womanly way. Even for lesbians it is often very difficult to detect another lesbian.

Before gathering in this and the following chapters more facts that give a true picture of the phenomenon of female homosexuality we cite an article a lesbian wrote for an American magazine[10]:

"I have always felt that the homosexual and the person who lives up to society's expectations could be friends if both would attempt to understand each other. I have had homosexual friends who, after suffering cruelty from normal persons who knew them—or knew of them—bitterly closed all doors to any except their own kind. I have seen homosexuals lose their jobs because someone discovered what they were and decided they might prove 'contagious'.

"On the other hand I have at least several normal friends who know all about me, and do not cringe at my touch. I wish there could be more of them—not only for myself but for other homosexuals. Eventually we wouldn't have to play 'hide-and-seek' with the world. One of the reasons I'm happy, I think, is because some of my dearest married friends neither pity nor hate me for being what I am. I haven't tried to lead them astray or break up their homes. I wouldn't—even if I thought I could do so. They are happy in being what they are. So am I. They can confide in me as 'woman to woman'. I can speak to their husbands as 'man to man'.

"But there are other friends and acquaintances with whom I will 'pass' as one of themselves, still 'waiting for the right man to come along'. I like them too, but I know that in order to keep them liking me, I'll make certain that my opinions and actions are carefully guarded. It is hard for me to dislike people and I do not willingly make an enemy . . .

"The idea of decent and happy normal people is universally accepted. But the decent and happy homosexual has not yet been accepted.

"If a great number of homosexuals are neurotic, an unsympathetic environment might have much to do with it. I am one of the rarely fortunate ones. No friend has ever betrayed me. I have had much of what I wanted. Yet I have suffered enough to realise how easily anyone under the same circumstances could become neurotic. I was never forced to marry. I was never spat upon and decried publicly in a small town as one of my friends was. I found myself, without living in puzzled bewilderment all of my life as to my true sexual identity. I knew what I wanted to be and I had the opportunity to be it.

"Undoubtedly some psychiatrists would blame my homosexuality on the fact that I spent my adolescence in a girls' school. Knowing the girls as I did, I know that such blame would be unjust. I never met one active homosexual there, though I was well acquainted with many of my classmates. Attending a girls' school did nothing to diminish my friends' ardour for the male, but rather doubled their intensity. I was about the only one who did not dedicate all conversations to the subject of boys. The girls were as odd to me then as I was to them. Today, nearly all of them are normal married people.

"It is true that I had no brothers and my father died before I could remember him very well. This might have fostered my homosexuality if it were not for the fact that some of my female homosexual friends had a father and often three or four brothers of whom they were very fond.

"However, I have little faith in the theory that all homosexuality is the product of environment. There are too many different environments including the perfectly normal one, which is as fertile a field for the homosexual as any other. I do not deny that some individuals can be influenced by some environments, but I doubt that all individuals react the same to all environments. That is why I believe a homosexual is 'born' more often than he is 'made' . . .

"I admit I have envied certain men because they had

102

wives. I have loved and wished that one of them could somehow be my own love forever. But I have never felt envy for any woman's husband, no matter how much I liked and respected him. Towards men I have felt and continue to feel a close kinship, a friendliness, but it has never gone deeper than that. To a woman I would give my entire heart as easily and as naturally as anything could be given.

"I do not feel as if my mind were 'sick or diseased'. I do not feel repressed or frustrated nor emotionally starved, nor that I am any of the terrible things that homosexuals are supposed to be. And yet, things have not always been as perfect in my life as I have longed for them to be—perhaps they never will be. But I have no regrets, for I have had some of the happiest of moments—days—years. And I am glad that I was born as a homosexual."

In a way these are pathetic words, written by a woman who knew the truth about herself and whose statement "I am glad that I was born as a homosexual" probably is only a childish way of suppressing a quite natural realisation of unhappiness and restlessness. Yet these are important words. They make us realise that we are talking in this book not about clinical theories and data, but about people, real people with thoughts, desires, fears and emotions of their own.

Lesbians are no freaks. The woman who wrote: ". . . things have not always been as perfect in my life as I have longed for them to be," is a homosexual, but in her heart dwells that eternal woman of whom Shakespeare wrote: "Age cannot wither her, nor custom stale her infinite variety".

1. Magnus Hirschfeld: *Die Homosexualität des Mannes und des Weibes*, Berlin 1914.

2. As cited by Kurt Dettmann: *Der Mann und die Lesbische Liebe* Hamburg 1963.

3. Joachim Pauly: *Eros auf falschem Wege*, Hamburg 1961.

4. Paul Reboux: *ABC de l'Amour*.

5. Noël Coward: *Palms, Pomp and Circumstance*.

6. Frank S. Caprio: *Female Homosexuality ; a Psychodynamic Study of Lesbianism*, New York 1954, London 1957.

7. Edmund Bergler: *Homosexuality, Disease or Way of Life?*, New York 1956. In this book the late Dr Bergler takes a very negative stand regarding male and female homosexuality. Donald Cory in his book *The Homosexual in America* (New York 1951) attacked Bergler for the still more negative point of view he expressed in his previous book *Neurotic Counterfeit-Sex* (New York 1951).

8. George W. Henry: *Sex Variants, a Study of Homosexual Patterns*, New York and London 1941.

9. *Dialoog, Tijdschrift voor Homofilie en Maatschappij*, 1965, No. 3. Published by Stichting Dialoog, Amsterdam, Holland.

10. Lorynca Rome: "I'm glad I'm a Homosexual" in *Sexology Magazine*, November 1950.

CHAPTER SEVEN

"A World They Never Made"

The aversion the public nurses in regard to male homosexuality resounded in the words Viscount Montgomery
spoke in the House of Lords when in June 1965 the Bill
of a new law on homosexual acts was discussed: "I regard the act of homosexuality in any form as the most
abominable bestiality that any human being can take part
in and which reduces him almost to the status of an animal. The proper title of this bill should be 'A Charter for
Buggery'." During these discussions Montgomery proposed
to guarantee men protection by law against homosexual
acts till they had reached their eightieth birthday!

In the course of these discussion nobody touched the
subject of female homosexuality. The reason is that British
legislation never mentions lesbianism. It is believed this was
because of the sensitiveness of nineteenth-century legislators
who did not want to hurt the feelings of prude Queen Vic-
toria, who simply could not believe such unspeakable things
occurred between women.

The legal discrimination made male homosexuality
go underground. Lesbianism stayed more or less in the
open. As a consequence the male homosexuals became a
persecuted minority with all the problems of such a group.
All too often members of a minority try to identify themselves with their group—which gets the look of a kind of
"secret society"—and consequently lose themselves in
vague ideas of being the chosen people that has to bring

salvation to a poor world. How many homosexual men are not sincerely convinced of being the sole heirs of the old Greek tradition?

Though lesbians cannot speak freely about their tastes and emotions, most of the time they do not suffer in the same way from this "minority complex". They are less organised, living a less subterranean existence than male homosexuals and having more ties with everyday life. Of course this does not mean they feel at home in a heterosexual world. To vary a verse of A. E. Housman, they are "lonely and afraid in a world they never made" and the document in Chapter 5 is there to prove it.

In the past medical researchers interested in lesbianism tried time and time again to classify female homosexuals, but almost every classification after some time had to be supplanted by a new one, as too many exceptions to the rule were found. It was the Viennese psychiatrist Sigmund Freud[1] who divided lesbians into the absolutely inverted type, that showed no interest in men and did not enjoy sexual relations with them, and the amphigonously inverted type—the "bisexual" who enjoys sexual relations with both sexes.

With regard to the second type it is interesting to find its place on the rating scale Alfred Kinsey composed. According to Kinsey a human being can be:

0. Exclusively heterosexual.

1. Predominantly heterosexual, only incidentally homosexual.

2. Predominently heterosexual, but more than incidentally homosexual.

3. Equally heterosexual and homosexual.

4. Predominantly homosexual, but more than incidentally heterosexual.

5. Predominantly homosexual, but incidentally heterosexual.

6. Exclusively homosexual.

We agree with Kinsey, that scientifically it is a necessity to make classifications when studying a certain subject; nevertheless it has proved to be very difficult and unsatisfactory when dealing with the human psyche. Psychologists have made classifications of all sorts, but I am sure that they never encountered a human being who fitted completely into one class. Only working theories have been provided.

As for lesbians, many attempts have been made at classification, but such attempts do not even provide a working theory. The reason is that there is too little factual material available to proceed upon. The average family doctor can only listen, when he has a patient who has difficulties that are caused by her lesbianism, because the subject is alien to him. He cannot put the right questions so it all remains very much on the surface. If the doctors of the world would relate their experiences to a central point for say ten years, maybe we could have a more or less reliable statistic to work with and to base a classification upon. As it is now all the existing classifications cannot pass the first test.

THE TWO FACES OF LESBIANISM

And yet there are two easily distinguishable types of lesbians—two types one also finds among male homosexuals: the masculine and the feminine. The masculine type always plays an active part in courting and love-making. The feminine type is the passive partner. In everyday life, the "dyke"—or "butch"—goes out into the hostile world to earn a living. Her partner stays at home and keeps house. Jane McKennon[2] writes about the typical "dyke" in an article and states she "is a large person, that is, tall although not necessarily heavy. She is successful in the business world. She is intelligent and uses her manly qualities to advance her in her work. Her clothes are good, she frequently wears tailored suits and dresses and does not care for fussy hair styles or frills of any kind. She is not drawn to another like herself because she is the aggressive sort whose efficiency and capability make her desire a partner who would be emotionally dependent on her. In many cases her behaviour with her friend can be likened to that of a mother with a helpless child."

It is among these masculine lesbians that we find the ones who like to dress and live as men. In every war several of the enemy soldiers who are brought to camps for prisoners of war turn out to be women in disguise. In a later chapter on the subject of lesbians in the army we will cite some case histories.

Hirschfeld relates an interesting case in Paris at the start of the century.

"The Paris correspondent of a Berlin newspaper reported: 'The archeologist Madame Dieulafoy, who directed the excavations at Susa, has received the president of the republic and his wife during their visit to the Louvre to inspect the treasures from the excavations, dressed in an elegant dress-suit, the ribbon of the "Legion d'Honneur" in her button-hole. Like a real cavalier, she offered Mme Carnot her arm while leading her around. At the academic dinner, given by M. and Mme. Dieulafoy, the lady, who seems to have changed her sex completely, had arranged it so that at her left and right side ladies were seated, while her husband, opposite her, did the same.' "

Dr Hirschfeld mentions a club in New York with members who were for the greater part female artists. In the luxuriously furnished rooms of this club, situated on one of the most fashionable avenues, men were under no circumstances admitted. The female members could only appear clad in men's attire, being free to modify it to their personal taste. Miss Jessie Bartlett-Davies wore a blue jacket with gilded buttons, and knickerbockers of the same hue, while Miss Edna Wallace Hopper, a brilliant comedy star, preferred a gold-coloured suit. Miss Ethel Barrymore wore loose-fitting trousers and light blouse; double-breasted suits were worn by Miss Josephine Hall and Miss Lilian Russell, performers at the operetta. The sculptors and painters among the members of the club used exclusively the traditional artist's costume of velvet and lustre; the painter Miss Edith Sarah Crowndale had a preference for a costume à la Canon, with jack-boots, in the club but also outside it.

Caprio in his book on lesbianism[3] states: "In Spain and Russia lesbians have been known to pass as men and were accepted for military service. It was only upon their death that their true identity became known. We are told that the famous painter of animals, Rosalie (Rosa) Bonheur frequently dressed as a man. George Sand, the French novelist, showed a definite preference for men's clothes. She was known to have occasionally smoked cigars and was nicknamed 'Monsieur Sand'."

The most famous of all male impostors was without doubt the mysterious Chevalier d'Eon.* Historians still are not sure if "he" was a woman who behaved, dressed and lived as a man and was at the end of her life forced to accept the fact she was a woman, or if he was a man who afterwards was forced to live and die as a woman. Anyhow the Chevalier d'Eon played a very important part in the political life of eighteenth-century France. To put it to an end he—or she—had to sign a statement that the so called Chevalier d'Eon had been a woman all his (her) life. Contemporaries stated his outward appearance was very striking and feminine. Everyone agrees "he" was of a fascinating female beauty. Casanova[4] wrote in his memoirs: "The King knew and had always known that d'Eon was a woman." Louis XV considered the complicated relations the Chevalier maintained with the Ministry

* For further details see John Davenport, *Aphrodisiacs and Love Stimulants with other Chapters on the Secrets of Venus.* Luxor Press, 9/6.

of Foreign Affairs—which did not suspect his true identity and employed him as a spy—as a private joke.

In his time the Chevalier was a very well-known and notorious personality and the lesbians of Paris who had joined forces in the secret society called the "Secte Anandryne" erected a statue in "her" honour in their "Temple of Vesta".

As for the feminine type of lesbian, nobody would suspect her of any homosexual tendencies. She lacks the masculine appearance and the aggressive attitude of the "dyke" and looks just like any other woman who has a heterosexual relationship. Sometimes these feminine lesbians look more feminine than the most feminine heterosexual! Very often this type is bisexual and the cause of her homosexual leanings is her need of motherly love, attention and affection. Like the feminine male homosexual she is fascinated by her own beauty. Richmond, who knew this type of lesbian very well, describes her as a girl "who bores her teachers by hanging around them and who is always seeking for physical contact with other girls and women, twining her arms about them, kissing them and fondling them; the girl who is often thought and spoken of by her elders as a 'little fool' without any realisation of the warped sexuality which is prompting her actions."

It is obvious that the mannish "Amazon"-type of lesbian feels attracted to the girlish, feminine type, not only because she likes to boss passive women, but also because in this type she finds the embodiment of the ideal of the eternal woman—an ideal she pursues in vain. Vice versa the feminine lesbian finds in the personality of the Amazon all those masculine characteristics she is longing for but which she will never possess. One can say that both types try to compensate in a relationship for characteristics they lack. The masculine woman adores the feminine; the feminine loves the masculine.

Of course it is wrong to believe that one type under all circumstances is bossed by the other. It is because of her feminine tricks and cunning that the passive type easily enslaves the masculine lesbian. As a matter of fact it is sometimes extremely difficult to distinguish the two types and to say exactly who is who.

Marika is a girl of twenty-one who looks like a boy of seventeen. She dresses in blue jeans, leather boots, cowboy shirt and a field jacket. She has her fair hair cut short and most people are surprised when they hear she is a girl. Her father is a well-known author. Her mother died when Marika was still a baby. Marika has the most ungirlish profession in the world. She is a souteneur and "owns" three or four prostitutes. Every night she takes her small red sports car and makes the rounds. She checks the customers and the earnings of her girls and raises hell if one of them had a slack day. All her girls are lesbians and Marika admits sexual relations with all of them but stresses the point there is no real love between her and her girls. Marikà has only one great love in her life: Anna. She shares with her an apartment and since she met her four years ago—Marika had run away from home and Anna took pity on her and afterwards fell in love with her —she has never left her.

Anna is in her forties and works as a civil servant. She is a big, stout woman but has a soft motherly personality. She never bosses Marika, yet she is always having her way. Marika likes to please her friend. She really loves her and as Anna loves her in return she puts up with Marika's remarkable profession—a profession, she realises, that could endanger her career as a civil servant if it became widely known.

Now it would be very difficult to call Marika a feminine girl. She is very masculine. Anna isn't very feminine either and has a rather masculine appearance that is stressed by the way she dresses.

One could say that Marika is attracted by her elder friend because unconsciously she is looking for the mother she lost when she was still a child. And maybe Anna has

111

found in Marika the love-hungry child she always has been looking for. In the case of Marika and Anna there is no masculine woman bossing a feminine one. There are just two women who are in need of each other because one of them wants to be loved and the other wants to love.

Edith is an artist. She draws illustrations for children's books and has a very successful career. She has the looks of a childish, young and innocent girl. Though she is twenty-six she dresses like a high-school student—bobby-soxes and all. She has an attractive, tanned face and never uses make-up. At the publishing house she works for, lots of young men make eyes at her and they are very disappointed when they hear Edith is not interested in men. The only human being in the world Edith is interested in is Josephine, an unsightly mousy girl of twenty-three. Josephine works in an office and for a year and a half has shared Edith's apartment. Edith loves her. She spends all her spare time with her friend. Edith is a feminine girl. Josephine is neither feminine nor masculine. She is just an inconspicuous, unattractive girl with no particular interests. If she had been heterosexual she would have been predestined as an old maid. It is not only in heterosexual relations that love is blind!

A good example of a relationship between a masculine and a feminine woman is the homosexual "marriage" of Hilde and Laura. Hilde comes up to the expectations the public has of a real dyke. She is a big, awe-inspiring woman with a booming voice, a deep chested laugh, a good-natured personality and traces of a moustache on her upper lip. She works as a private secretary for an office manager who is a homosexual himself. Hilde wears very masculine suits, smokes cigars and likes the company of men. She never uses make-up and has her hair cut short. Most people who have to deal with her are afraid of her and look at her as something of a freak till they discover how efficiently Hilde works and what a wonderful personality she has.

For eight years Hilde has been "married" to Laura, an attractive, very feminine office girl. Though Laura has to work all day, she keeps house. At the end of the day she hurries home to dust the apartment and cook a meal for her and her friend. After dinner Hilde reads the paper and watches television—she has a preference for boxing— while Laura washes up.

It is Hilde who makes the decisions and who invites friends for a visit. She pays the bills and has the money both partners bring in under control. Their relationship is a clear example of a homosexual "marriage" in which one partner plays the part of the "husband" and the other one of the "wife".

Most of the relationships between lesbians do not last more than one or two years. As is the case with "marriages" between homosexual men, after some time the partners lose interest and drift away in new relationships.

This inconstancy is one of the main reasons heterosexuals look down upon homosexual relationships. But is a heterosexual lover really more faithful than a homosexual one? As long as two people—heterosexual or homosexual—love each other they are faithful. As soon as love ends both partners are getting interested in other men and women. When this happens a homosexual "marriage" breaks up, and each partner goes his way. On the contrary the heterosexual marriage can exist a long time—and sometimes all the time—without being fed with love. Why? The reason is of course that it is much easier to break up a homosexual relationship than a heterosexual marriage. A relationship between two lesbians or between two homosexual men is not the same as a civil marriage and needs not to be divorced. There are no children to be reckoned with and one need not to defy the opinion of family and friends. Imagine a society in which a heterosexual marriage could be dissolved as soon as one of the partners left the house and started somewhere else a new relationship. Imagine that there would be no children to take care of and no alimony to pay. Imagine nobody had to be ashamed in the eyes of friends and relatives of breaking up his or her marriage. How many men and women who stay together all their life now would do the same under those conditions? It is just circumstances that keep together a lot of married heterosexual people in our society! As long as we remember that there is no danger of looking down upon the "inferior" and "less devoted" relationships of homosexuals. Never forget that in every marriage after some time a crisis arises between the partners and it is mostly because of the responsibility with regard to the children that the marriage continues and both partners save the relationship by adapting themselves. If a homosexual relationship is hit by a crisis there is nothing that can save it except the responsibility of one partner for the other, and if love has disappeared it is very difficult to feel such a responsibility and maintain the relationship.

... AND SO TO BED

Male pride of the sexual organ fed the opinion that of two lesbians who make love to each other, one has to play the part of a male and consequently has to be in the possession of a penis to give the partner sexual satisfaction. Hard core pornography teems with scenes of lesbians making love by means of a dildo and in the public mind the dyke always has to make use of a skilfully-handled false penis to imitate coition and reach orgasm.

Of course the masculine type of lesbian wants to play a masculine part in love-making and therefore needs a passive partner. "I think it would be unnatural," said one dyke when asked if she would like to make love with another lesbian of the active masculine type.

Playing the active part in love-making does not mean however that the use of a dildo is indispensable. It is the

114

lesson of heated descriptions of lesbian love-play in porno-graphic novels like *Gamiani*[5]—written for heterosexual males! —that gave the public a false picture of the be-haviour of two lesbians in bed. Of course dildoes are used, but most of the times in brothels and during carefully staged performances for a male heterosexual audience. The use of the dildo in lesbian love suffers from the same misconception as the frequency with which anal inter-course is practised by male homosexuals. They are both the most sensational manifestations of homosexual love life and both extremely disgusting for the outside world. In reality the number of lesbians that make use of a false penis is as low as the number of male homosexuals who practise anal intercourse.

Of course lesbian love-making is more than the inno-cent fondling and kissing that the public pictures when thinking of two women in love with each other.

Most lesbians get sexual satisfaction by practising cun-nilingus: the kissing and stimulating of the clitoris by the mouth. Where one of the partners does not like the prac-tice, stimulation by hand takes over. The masculine type of lesbian makes the overtures and takes the lead in love-making. In some cases the feminine partner is not as pas-sive as imagined and after some time takes over the initiative.

We have already mentioned the novel *Fanny Hill*,* and for a description of a lesbian seduction-scene we now turn to that famous book. The naïve Fanny, newly arrived in London and unbeknown to herself in a bawdy-house, is the bedmate of another girl inmate:

Still blushing at now seeing myself naked to my shift, I hurried to get under the bedclothes out of sight. Phœbe

* The illustrated paperback edition is published by Luxor Press at 9/6.

laugh'd and it was not long before she placed herself by my side . . .

No sooner then was this precious substitute of my mistress's laid down, but she, who was never out of her way when any occasion of lewdness presented itself, turned to me, embraced and kiss'd me with great eagerness. This was new, this was odd; but imputing it to nothing but pure kindness, which, for aught I knew, it might be the London way to express in that manner, I was determin'd not be behind-hand with her, and returned her the kiss and embrace, with all the fervour that perfect innocence knew.

Encouraged by this, her hands became extremely free, and wander'd over my whole body, with touches, squeezes, pressures they either shock'd or alarm'd me.

The flattering praises she intermingled with these invasions contributed also not a little to bribe my passiveness; and, knowing no ill, I feared none, especially from one who had prevented all doubt of her womanhood, by conducting my hands to a pair of breasts that hung loosely down, in a size and volume that full sufficiently distinguished her sex, to me at least, who had never made any other comparison.

I lay then all tame and passive as she could wish, whilst her freedom raised no other emotions but those of a strange, and, till then, unfelt pleasure. Every part of me was open and exposed to the licentious courses of her hands, which, like a lambent fire, ran over my whole body, and thaw'd all coldness as they went.

In the meantime, the extension of my limbs, languid stretchings, sighs, short heavings, all conspired to assure that experienced wanton that I was more pleased then offended at her proceedings, which she seasoned with repeated kisses and exclamations . . .

For my part, I was transported, confused, and out of myself; feelings so new were too much for me. My heated and alarm'd senses were in a tumult that robbed me of

116

all liberty of thought; tears of pleasure gush'd from my eyes, and somewhat assuaged the fire that rag'd all over me.

OTHER MANIFESTATIONS OF LESBIAN LOVE

Of course stimulation of the clitoris by hands or mouth is not the only way lesbians reach orgasm. Next to cunnilingus there is anilingus and next to mutual masturbation there is, for the sado-masochistically inclined, mutual flogging. The part sado-masochism can play in lesbian relationships will be reviewed in a later chapter.

We have stated that the part the dildo plays in lesbian love-making is very small. Then why is the false penis such a popular subject in sexual folklore? Numerous are the jokes about this instrument and no self-respecting pornographer ever wrote at some time or another a book in which the dildo did not play an important part.

One of the reasons is, as we saw, the often childish pride men have in their own penis. Most of them are sure no lesbian love-play is ended by mutual orgasm if a clever imitation of their precious organ does not take part in the operation. But there is still another reason. False penises are manufactured in countries like Japan, Germany and the United States and they are sold. Dildoes do exist. But in most cases they are not bought by homosexual women to give their partners sexual satisfaction. Most of the instruments come into the hands of lonesome women. It is the spinster, the widow and the frustrated housewife who finds a solitary pleasure in the use of this instrument that is in some form virtually as old as mankind.

Love-play between two homosexual women sometimes takes shapes that are difficult to recognise as manifestations of mutual love.

Frieda was twenty-six years old when she came to me to ask advice. Though she was still young she had already

117

three or four relationships behind her. The reason all these love-affairs ended rather soon—not one lasted more than a year—was that no partner was able to give Frieda all the sexual satisfaction she wanted.

"In the beginning there are no difficulties. I'm so very glad I've found a new love that I wouldn't dream of making any demands on my partner. But after some weeks there is a change. Suddenly I lose interest in ordinary love-play. Suddenly I long for the extreme, the bizarre and the unusual. My partner thinks it's just a caprice and I have my way. After some time she discovers I'm making more and more demands on her with regard to love-making and that is the moment she's losing her interest in me . . ." Sadly she shook her head. "Then I'm soon as lonely again as I was before . . ."

I looked at her. She was a big, rather heavily built blonde with large green eyes in a remarkably handsome face. Frieda was a striking woman and I imagined it would be rather easy for her to find a partner who was looking for a friend of the masculine type, as she was much more attractive than the average dyke.

"What kind of demands do you make?" I probed carefully.

She shrugged her shoulders and I noticed she tried to dodge the answer.

"Oh, nothing in particular . . . I've got scenes in my imagination I try to realise . . ."

"What kind of scenes?"

Frieda sighed.

"As I said, nothing in particular . . ."

"Then why do your partners rebel?"

She smiled at me.

"They rebel, don't they? I guess that's the right word . . ." Again she shrugged. "Maybe they are right . . . Maybe my wishes are a little bit too far out . . ."

She stopped and I waited patiently. I was sure she was going to tell me everything.

118

"First it's the kisses . . ." she said thoughtfully. "I like to kiss in front of a mirror . . . Oh, nobody cares about that! Then I want to be caressed with a peacock's tail . . ." She smiled. "A bit *outré*, that wish, but I don't think you could call it repulsive, could you?'

"And after that?" I asked. "What's next? There must be a reason up till now why all your friends have left you."

She looked at me silently and then said quietly:

"Don't you worry. There is a reason . . . You know, I think it's the knife that scares them.'

"Which knife?'

"That big, sharp and shiny carving-knife. Of course it's just part of the game. I wouldn't be able to kill anybody. Really, I wouldn't, but I don't think they understand . . ." She shook her head sadly.

"It is you who handles the knife?' I probed again.

"Yes, but as I said, it's all part of the game. I really wouldn't be able to . . ." She looked at me intently, "It's a game called 'executioner's victim' . . . She has to be the victim. I'm the executioner and I'm all dressed in black. I wear a black hood too . . . First there has to be green light in the bedroom. I'm very peculiar about that, you know . . . Then my friend has to undress and after that is done I tie her to a bedpost in a fashion that she cannot see the door. After that I leave the room and she has to be alone for ten minutes or an hour. That depends, you know . . . Then very softly I enter. I don't want her to hear me, for in that case the game is up. Very softly I sneak up to her. The carving-knife is in my right hand. Then I jump and with my knife I cut her arm or her leg. As soon as there's blood I kiss her passionately . . ."

I didn't answer. She looked at me curiously and asked: "Do you think that could be the reason my friends keep away after some time? Do you think it's the knife that scares them? Of course I wouldn't dream of killing them, but I don't think they know . . ."

I looked at her gravely.

"I think it's the knife," I said. "It's both the knife and your behaviour that frightens them . . . I think most women don't like things like that in a relationship."

She thought that over. Suddenly something seemed to enter her mind. Something she never thought of before. There was anxiety in her voice when she said:

"Doctor . . . I . . . I know you're right . . . Now please be honest . . . Do you think I've . . . I've something of a sadist in me?"

I looked at her gravely and nodded.

"Yes, Frieda," I said.

NOTES

1. Sigmund Freud: "The Psychogenesis of a case of homosexuality in a woman" in *Collected Papers*, London 1924.

2. Jane McKennon: "I'm a homosexual woman" in *The Homosexuals*, New York 1954.

3. Frank S. Caprio: *Female Homosexuality a Psychodynamic study of Lesbianism*, New York 1954, London 1957.

4. Historians suppose Casanova here stated something that everybody in his surroundings knew. For his contemporaries there was nothing sensational about his statement.

5. Recently republished by the Cercle du Livre Precieux in Paris.

CHAPTER EIGHT

Lesbian Priestesses of Venus

Why does a woman become a prostitute?

There are about as many answers to that question as there are women who sell their love in the back-streets of the world's capitals. Every prostitute has her own tragic story of her life, that is calculated to move the hearts and purses of her customers.

"I'm doing this dirty work—if you can call it work—because I have a child. My little daughter is at a very expensive boarding-school and of course she doesn't know how her mother earns a living. When she's older I want her to study law. I know it will cost an awful lot of money, but I'm going to earn it with my own body. I'll do anything for my little darling. Only the best is good enough for her."

That is a very popular life-story. Sometimes the version is a little different. She doesn't have a daughter then, but is the mother of a son. Her darling has to study medicine, "to compensate for the things I did wrong. Yes sir, my boy is going to be a doctor."

Of course it is a heart-breaking story, but sad to say it is not a true story. Psychoanalysts discovered that often prostitutes became prostitutes not because their children need the best education there is, but because they are lesbians. And the children of prostitutes exist in most cases only in the imagination of the would-be mothers.

I realise this is a remarkable statement. To understand the motives of a prostitute, it is useful to have a look at the behaviour of their male counterparts: the men who conquer one woman after the other. Great lovers like Casanova and Don Juan suddenly lost their halo when modern psychoanalysts developed a theory that they probably were men with latent homosexual tendencies, who just wanted to prove time and time again to themselves that they were real he-men who could court women and satisfy them sexually.

Don Juan a latent homosexual? Is that not a little bit too far out?

Not if one realises that this theory solves a fascinating mystery in the life of this man and also reveals a motive that drove Casanova from one woman to another.

It is clear that both men met during their lives one or two women who could give them anything they needed and that could have made them happy. One has only to read Casanova's memoirs[1] to realise that. Then why did they leave these women just as they left all the others and go on hunting for new pretty faces and new conquests?

They did it just to make sure that they were normal heterosexual men and that this strange homosexual tendency they felt in their souls just did not exist. A few days spent in the company of one and the same woman gave them doubts already about their potency, prestige and ability to love. It is easy to court a woman, conquer her and satisfy her, if both partners consider such an event as just another adventure. However, it is much more difficult to conquer and satisfy the same woman for a second, a third and a fourth time. Then it is no longer the body that does all the work; heart and mind have to participate as well.

Don Juan and Casanova knew that. They had realised that they were not able to do this and it was the reason for their doubts. This is much more easy to understand if one knows that one of the great attractions Casanova had for women was the fact that he bathed regularly and consequently did not smell. And this in an era in which men were convinced of the bad influence water had on a person's health. Nobody washed his face. At the royal courts men and women perfumed themselves heavily to drown their body odours. The wigs these people wore, were not the immaculate white objects one sees in movies about the period; they swarmed with lice!

It is understandable that a man like Casanova who was clean and did not smell, attracted women, but it is also clear that his clean linen and the absence of a smell were no basis for a happy and lasting relationship.

Now we know that history's Great Lovers were very poor lovers who only wanted to prove their masculinity, it is much more easy to understand why such a great percentage of the world's prostitutes are lesbians.

PROSTITUTES ARE FRIGID WOMEN

Again a rather sensational statement and maybe a disappointment for regular customers of the world's temples of Venus. But here is the truth, straight from the horse's mouth: "Actually of course, despite all the feigned transports of ecstasy (for purposes of increasing the tip) to ninety-nine out of a hundred girls, going to bed with a customer is a joyless, even distasteful, experience." Polly Adler, formerly Madam of a very famous American brothel, made that statement in her autobiography *A House is Not A Home*.[2]

Now it is a well-known fact that women who cannot reach orgasm in sexual contact with men, turn to their own kind and become lesbians. One could not call them born lesbians. Their frigidity towards men turned them into lesbians. As the greater part of prostitutes are frigid, it is clear they have to turn to their own sex to find sexual satisfaction. Women who take this step form one group of lesbian prostitutes.

However, there is a—probably very large—second group.

123

It exists of women who have latent homosexual tendencies which they try to repress. They have much the same attitude as history's Great Lovers: by proving to themselves that they are wanted by men, that they can go to bed with men and that they can give men sexual satisfaction. Of course they get no sexual satisfaction themselves and after some time they turn to lesbian practices "to get something out of sex". The repression of their latent homosexuality lessens and within a few years they are straight lesbians. Those of them who still will not admit their lesbian tendencies pull the wool over their own eyes.

Files of sexologists like Hirschfeld[3], Wilhelm Stekel[4] and Albert Moll[5] are full of case-histories of women who earned their living as prostitutes while being lesbians. Some cases make it clear that these lesbian prostitutes sometimes hate men and only put up with them because it is their only way of earning a living.

Quite a number of years ago I met a lesbian who was a prostitute. Her name was Paula and she shared her apartment with another lesbian, Ilse, who was also a prostitute. Both girls were very happy together and they had one thing in common: they both detested men.

"They're just animals," Paula said to me. "Big brutes who can think of one thing only: sex. They have no understanding for the subtle workings of a woman's mind. As a matter of fact I don't think they are interested at all in the mind of a woman. They just want her body."

"Being a prostitute, I'm afraid on this point you're liable to be prejudiced," I told her.

She shrugged.

"Maybe. All I can tell you is that every experience I've had with men points in the same way."

"Of course," I said patiently. "Please don't forget they all come to you with the same thing in mind! "

"That's not what I mean." She shook her head. "I haven't always been a prostitute! I've known men when I was young and they were the same brutes as the ones that

124

pay me money now for the most outrageous debaucheries."

"Tell me about those early experiences, Paula."

"Why should I? It's all over and done with. Who is interested in what happened twenty or thirty years ago?"

"I am," I told her. "And if I know about it, I can help you . . ."

"Who needs help?" she sneered.

"You do," I said gently. "I suppose that's the reason you came to see me."

"Don't you think I'm unhappy, doctor! Ilse and I are devoted to each other. We love each other and we try to make a success of our relationship! I really am very happy. I wouldn't be anything but a lesbian. It's just . . ."

"It's just that you hate the way you have to earn a living. You detest men and I can imagine it must be ghastly for you to be at their beck and call! It must be horrible for you to perform the most revolting actions, just to satisfy the sexual needs of creatures you hate!"

She nodded.

"That's right. I'll be honest with you. Ilse and I nurse our money. We live very economically, forever trying to postpone the day one of us has to go out on the streets and find a few customers . . ."

"I understand you work in turns?"

"Yes. Last time I was the one who had to bring home the money. At this moment Ilse is out on the streets . . ." She bit her lip and looked at me pleadingly. "Oh, doctor, you'll have to help me . . . I can't stand it any longer . . . Really, Ilse and I, we're very happy . . . and yet . . . I've thought of suicide . . . You know at the end of a night in which I go to bed with six or seven men, I . . . I . . . detest myself!"

"I'll do my best to help you, Paula," I said. "But when you're going to be my patient we have to trust each other. Is that clear?"

Again she nodded.

125

"Yes, doctor. I know what you mean. You want me to tell the truth . . . the whole truth and nothing but the truth. Is that it?" She looked at me as if she were right. "I hope my story won't disappoint you. You know, I'm a very simple girl with a very simple background . . ."

"Maybe that will make it easier for both of us, Paula," I said encouragingly.

Listening to the story of Paula's life I realised there must be thousands and thousands of women like her. She was born in a small village. Her father was a fisherman. Her mother worked as a seamstress. Both parents had to work hard and neither of them found time to show some interest in their children. Paula had an older sister. As they were very poor that girl soon had to leave the house and earn a living as a maid. Most of the time Paula was alone.

She went to school and when she was fourteen she was raped by the local drunk. It was a thing of no importance in this backward village but on Paula it made a lasting impression.

"You know, doctor," she said pensively. "There are nights I still dream of that man. Then I can smell his stinking breath and feel his hairy hands on my body. Isn't that strange after all these years and after having given myself to hundreds of men?"

When the rapist made her his victim Paula knew almost nothing about sex. Her parents were ashamed of what had happened. They did not tell the girl exactly what had happened to her, but sent her to a woman, a welfare worker, who lived in the city and who promised to keep Paula with her till "the scandal had blown over".

"And then a most unexpected thing happened to me," Paula said. "I fell in love with that woman. I was fourteen and she must have been around thirty . . . She wasn't married. These welfare workers almost never are. I think she cared a lot for me, but I don't think she was a lesbian.

126

Maybe she had always longed for a daughter like me . . .
I don't know. But I loved her."

"Maybe you projected the love you had for your mother
on her," I said. "After all your mother never found time
to show any interest in you . . ."

"I don't know . . ." She shrugged. "I only know I loved
her. Maybe it is true what you said. Maybe I loved her as
a child loved her mother, but it wasn't all that. I'm quite
sure there was also another kind of love . . . I imagine that
love resembled in a way the feelings young girls foster for
their teacher . . . You know, one always hears about girls
who fall head over heels in love with a handsome teacher.
I think in my case it was the same kind of love . . . Only I
didn't fall in love with a man . . . I fell in love with a
woman."

"Did she know?"

"Yes, I think she did, but she must have thought it was
only a caprice of a child. She didn't pay any attention to it
and that made it worse."

"Then what happened?"

"A few months later I had to go home again. It was a
catastrophe." She was silent.

"Why, Paula?" I gently probed. "What happened?"

"I wasn't happy any more. I didn't feel at home any
more. I longed for . . . her. Her kisses, her embraces,
her attention . . . her love. I tried to tell my father and
my mother, but they didn't understand. I think they too
saw only a childish caprice in it. Then I ran away from
home."

"Yes, I did. How did you guess?" She looked at me
curiously. "My comeback wasn't a big success. She took
the first train to bring me home again. My parents were
furious. Father beat me . . . Then they decided I was
old enough to work and told me to find a job as a
maid."

"And you found yourself a job?"

She shook her head and smiled.

127

"No, I didn't. Again I ran away from home, but this time I didn't go to the woman I loved, though I did go to the city. I told myself that if I had to look for a job, I would choose one that was easy and that would give me the opportunity to earn a lot of money I could keep for myself. I don't think it was such a bad idea. Why should I give money to my parents? They meant nothing to me. There was nothing I had to be thankful for . . ." Again silence.

I waited.

Paula looked up, smiled an apologetic smile and said:

"I became a prostitute. Of course it wasn't that simple. I started as a kind of lone wolf . . . walking through the city . . . offering myself to passers-by. I bet most of them didn't understand what I wanted, I was still such a child . . . But some older gentlemen got the message . . . I had to go with them and they gave me money. For some weeks I lived in the house of one of them . . . He was nice to me, but his tastes were degenerate, to say the least. He must have known I was only fifteen, for he never allowed me to leave the house. Then one night he told me it was too dangerous to keep such a young girl hidden and he turned me out. It was winter and terribly cold. I thought I would die . . . Then an older woman found me and took me home. She turned out to be the owner of a notorious brothel, now of course disappeared. It appeared that some of her regular customers like their prostitutes fresh . . ." She smiled. "Let's say I was in great demand."

Paula told me what they wanted her to do during the long sweaty days and nights in that brothel and I shivered. I thought of that small girl that was being depraved by roués; of the unscrupulous Madam who used her to earn money —a lot of money—for the "special services" rendered.

"I think you could call me the child prodigy of the bawdy-house," Paula said reflectively. "It lasted only one or two years. Then I looked more than my age and the child prodigy was finished. I wasn't happy but I didn't

128

know where to go or what to do . . . So I stayed in that
brothel and then one day everything changed when I met
Lili. She was older than me and in a way she reminded me
of my first love, the welfare worker. We became friends
and very soon I found I loved her. Lili told me she loved
me . . ."

"Did the others know about your love?"

She nodded.

"It soon became known that we were lovers . . . That
was the reason we left the brothel . . ." She must have seen
astonishment on my face, for she smiled and said: "Oh no!
Don't think we were ashamed that the others knew! We
couldn't care less! It was just that the Madam tried to
make use of it."

"I don't understand what you mean, Paula."

She looked at me compassionately.

"Don't you really? I thought doctors knew life! Oh,
you must know there are people who like to see lesbians
make love! Every brothel had customers with tastes that
went in that direction. And don't you think they were
always men! I've seen women and married couples among
my audience . . . For a good fee we put on the 'Grand
Spectacle'—that's how it was called. It was a performance
of a lesbian orgy that lasted about three-quarters of an
hour. A number of girls—and sometimes one or two men
if a customer insisted on it—figured in it. The audience
could state what kind of things it wanted to see: cunnilingus, anilingus, masturbation, fellatio, anything you like.
Of course we had to take part in these performances—they
belonged to the daily occurrences in a big bawdy-house—
but as soon as the Madam learned of our relationship she
wanted Lili and me to put on a special act. An act of two
women who were so much in love with each other that
they completely forgot the audience and lost themselves in
the most refined love play, complete with dildoes and all the
other contraptions the man in the street associates with
lesbianism."

129

"Then what did you do?"

"Oh, I think we still had some decency left, for we told her: Thank you very much, but if you think we're going to put on a circus like that, you're sadly mistaken."

"She didn't like that, I suppose?"

"You judge of the human mind, you! You bet she didn't like it! Five minutes later we were out in the street and that was the start of our partnership. We found an apartment and set up our household . . ."

There was nothing unique in the life of Paula. I had heard the same story many times. Parents who are too poor and too busy to take interest in their children; a child that is raped and afterwards falls in love with a mother's substitute.

The life in a brothel and the "Grand Spectacles"—I had heard it many, many times during a long career. It was just the life of the average old prostitute. After a treatment that took much time and trouble I succeeded in taking away the hatred Paula felt towards men. Afterwards they just left her cold, and making love to them was only a very boring experience. It was all I could do for her . . .

FOR LESBIANS ONLY

In most of the capitals of the world one can find the bars and street-corners where homosexuals can make their choice out of a number of male prostitutes. These prostitutes come in all kinds: the "he-man", the feminine man, the soldier, the sailor and the tough guy with his leather jacket. One by one they are clichés, but that is what their customers want them to be. It is obvious that there is a similar trade in lesbian prostitutes. Here too we find the clichés: the very feminine girl and the big masculine woman, the typical "outdoor girl" and the "butch", sometimes complete with motor-cycle.

Most of these prostitutes are free-lancers. They keep

the money they earn for themselves. However, it is different in some big cities where brothels are still to be found that cater especially to lesbian tastes.

Here a lesbian with enough money to spend can make her choice. The Madam of the house gives an order for a "parade" and a long row of girls passes the female customer who is seated in an easy chair. As soon as she has found what she is looking for, there is a talk about money. A price is fixed and the customer disappears with her favourite into one of the rooms.

A great number of these lesbian brothels have the same wealthy and refined interiors as their heterosexual counterparts. There is a library with obscene novels on the theme of lesbianism, on the walls there are etchings taken from an illustrated edition of *Gamiani* and there are special rooms for customers who have a taste for flagellation or want to practise the use of a false penis.

Many married women with homosexual tendencies who are afraid to look for a female friend make use of these brothels. Great care is taken to keep the identity of every visitor secret. Lesbian brothels are much more discreetly run than heterosexual bawdy-houses and that is the reason the public hardly knows of their existence.

Male homosexuals often complain that a great number of male prostitutes to be found in our big cities are not homosexual at all, but heterosexual and bent on easy money. The same phenomenon is seen in lesbian prostitution. As pointed out already a great number of prostitutes with male customers are lesbians and some of the prostitutes for lesbians are heterosexual!

The reason for this strange phenomenon is that the heterosexual prostitutes for lesbians are recruited from two groups of women. The first are those who feel ashamed to be a "real" prostitute. They are convinced that going to bed with a woman is not as bad as going to bed with a man. Some of them even think it has not got anything to do with sex at all.

131

The second group consists of women who do not like to take chances. Being an ordinary prostitute has its risks. One can be robbed, even killed and there is always the danger of a baby and consequently of an expensive abortion.

All these risks are avoided by the prostitute who offers her services to lesbians. Some prostitutes have male as well as female clients. The way such a prostitute is contacted by a lesbian is described in the closing chapter of an American novel on the theme of lesbianism: [6]

"The phone rang twice. Then a cool female voice spoke along the wire. 'Hello?'

Ronni swallowed. 'Am I talking to Cindy?'

'Yes, this is she.'

'I was put in touch with you by a mutual friend—a cab driver. He—explained the nature of your services, and the fee——'

The voice paused. 'I see.'

'Is there—any chance that you might be free this evening?'

'Yes. I'm free.'

'Good.'

'Do you have the address?'

'Yes.' Ronni thought for a moment. '78B, is that right?'

'Yes.'

'Thank you very much.'

'Miss?' Cindy's voice had an odd sound to it.

'What is it?'

'May I ask for whom you are requesting the services?'

Ronni struggled to keep her voice calm. 'For myself.'

The pause this time was almost eternal. 'I see,' she said at last.

'Is . . . is that all right?'

'Yes. The fee is one hundred dollars.'

'I know.'

'Very well. When shall I expect you?'

132

'In just a few minutes. I'm right across the street.'

'Ring the bell twice if you would.'

'Certainly. Whatever you say.'

She started to hang up, but once again Cindy's voice came across the wire. 'Miss?'

'Yes?'

'Could you tell me your name? Just your first name of course. I think we should be on a friendly basis, business notwithstanding.'

'Veronica. But my friends call me Ronni.'

'Ronni.' A pause. 'I shall be expecting you.'

The line went dead."

For many normal heterosexual women lesbianism is a piquant adventure; a sensation they undergo at a wild party when everyone has had too much to drink and a few girls with homosexual tendencies lose their self-control. For many heterosexual men lesbianism plays an important part in their sex life. Countless men have fantasies of lesbian women making love to each other. Pornographic pictures and movies with scenes of lesbian love-making sell extremely well. Why? These men who order in a brothel a "Grand Spectacle" and who buy pictures and movies with lesbian scenes, would not dream of marrying a lesbian. They even would not dream of making love with one. Then why are they interested in lesbians? In a later chapter we shall try to answer that question.

Of cour e it is wrong to think that prostitution is a well-known phenomenon among lesbians. Most lesbians never had anything to do with prostitutes and prostitution. By far the majority of them are hard-working women who realise that in a way they are different and who try to live with that knowledge. They make friends the same way as other people do: at parties, during work, in a shop, in a street or at the office. Their feelings for the one they love can be as profound as those a heterosexual woman cherishes for the man she loves.

133

A great number of lesbians who live in a happy relationship with a partner, would like to have children. It is the knowledge that they never will have one that sometimes makes them sad. Nevertheless in many countries one or two children are allotted to the mother when a married lesbian divorces her husband. The only thing of importance in that case is a certainty that these children are going to live in balanced surroundings, that they are going to be loved and that the mother and her friend will do anything that is in their power to make them happy.

I know two lesbians who live together with the little daughter of one of them. In this case the mother was not divorced, but her husband died a few years after the child was born. At that moment this woman already had a lesbian relationship with an unmarried woman of her own age. Some time after the death of the husband the friend moved into the house and since that day the three of them have been very happy. The little girl is the pivot on which everything hinges. Both women are going to tell her all about their relationship as soon as the child is old enough to understand and they both want to point out to her then that the relationship her mother has is an exception.

"I really hope she'll marry a man and be happy with him and have children," the mother told me. "I know that I have been lucky . . . I had a loving husband, a child I adore and now I have my friend . . . Things could have been different . . . I've seen too many lonely and desperate lesbians to think that I belong to a chosen people . . . We'll do everything to turn our little girl into a normal woman with normal feelings. There's only one thing I'm not sure about . . . I wonder what she'll think and say about her mother when she is grown up and has children of her own . . ."

134

1. Now published in a new and finally complete and unexpurgated edition by Brockhaus Verlag in Wiesbaden.

2. Polly Adler: *A House is not a Home*, New York 1953.

3. Magnus Hirschfeld: *Jahrbücher für Sexuelle Zwischenstufen*, Leipzig. After 1898 several yearbooks were published.

4. Wilhelm Stekel: *Onanie und Homosexualität*, Berlin 1923.

5. Albert Moll: *Die Konträre Sexualempfindung*, Berlin 1899.

6. Jessie Dumont: *Made in Hell*, New York 1962.

CHAPTER NINE

Prison and the Services—Paradise
for Lesbians

As soon as many women are brought together and deprived of every contact with men, lesbianism rears it head. Quite naturally this is a consequence of the fact that normal heterosexual women, if sex starved, turn to each other to realise their sexual tensions. When a great number of women are brought together it is quite obvious that there are many potential and straight lesbians among them.

To prisons or army camps for women, other lesbians are attracted. In prisons for women they try to find work as matrons. As for the army's women corps, here they enlist to be among other female homosexuals.

Due to these factors female homosexuality in prisons and in the army is a big headache for the authorities. Up till now no one has been able to find an infallible way of fighting it. It is not the fact that in prisons and in army corps lesbians have an opportunity of meeting each other that worries the authorities. Much more important—and disastrous—is the phenomenon that lots of normal, heterosexual women undergo lesbian experiences while in prison and cannot find satisfaction any more in a heterosexual love-life after they are released. As was stated in preceding chapters, a great number of prostitutes are lesbians. In countries where prostitution is punishable under the law, prostitutes are imprisoned and consequently brought into contact with other women. However, this is

136

not the only danger that threatens the inmates of prisons. Joan Henry, who wrote a book about life in a women's prison,[1] did not mince matters when she stated: "Unfortunately a great many women who are attracted to the prison service are themselves lesbians and it can and does do a great deal of harm if they focus their attention on some of the prisoners, particularly the young girls (who are obviously the first choice)." According to this author some of the liaisons that started in prison between gaoler and prisoner become permanent when the prison sentence is finished. As for the importance of lesbianism in prisons, an American authority[2] gave it as his opinion that there were more female homosexuals in women's prisons than outside.

Lesbianism is quite an ordinary phenomenon in prisons. Joan Henry put it this way in her book: " 'Well, I suppose there is bound to be a lot of homosexuality in prisons,' said I, beginning to undress. 'Omo wot?—Come off it, ducks—lesbians—that's wot they call 'em 'ere.' "

To give a clear picture of the influence lesbian experiences gained in prison can have on a woman's psyche, here follows the case history of Mitzi. She used to work as a teacher in an elementary school and had to serve a sentence for the embezzlement of funds of a women's club she belonged to. It was a rather tragic case as Mitzi used the money to pay the costs of an operation her mother had to undergo.

When she went to prison to serve a sentence of six months, she was twenty-eight and engaged to be married.

"MARLENE MUST HAVE HYPNOTISED ME..."

"Paul, my fiancée, said goodbye to me when I went to prison . . . I cried and asked him to wait for me. Half a year isn't that long, I told him . . . Paul told me he loved me and promised to wait for me and to meet me at the prison

137

entrance when my sentence was finished. Little did I know then that six months later everything would be different and that I would have lost all interest in him . . ."

"Did Paul visit you while you were in prison?"

"Once or twice. You see, he works as an engineer on construction work and before long he was sent quite some distance away."

"Did you like those visits?"

"Oh yes! It broke the routine of prison life."

I looked at her attentively.

"You already had met Marlene?"

She nodded.

"Yes, I had . . . At first I had to get accustomed to my new way of life. You've got no idea what it means to be in prison, doctor . . . You've to forget all your old values and standards . . . and of course you've to swallow your pride . . . I was put in a prison that was very crowded and we had to sleep with two or three women in one cell. Marlene and I shared one cell and I think that was my undoing . . . At first nothing happened . . . Later it became different . . ."

"Who was Marlene?" I asked. Mitzi was a beautiful girl with nice blue eyes and fair hair that she wore long. She was of medium height and had an intelligent face. I wondered what kind of woman Marlene must have been.

"Ah! Who was Marlene? It is not easy to answer that question, doctor! Marlene became my best friend . . . my lover. Yes, I think I can easily say I loved her . . . She wasn't only my best friend but also in a way my mother . . ." She looked at me sternly. "Please don't laugh about that. I mean it. I don't think my mother ever cared for me like Marlene did." She smiled. "She was very jealous! You should have seen her face when other inmates tried to make passes at me! "

"What kind of a girl was she?"

"Oh, I know I'm going to shock you now! Maybe you'll be disgusted . . ."

I smiled.

"I'm used to being shocked, Mitzi."

"All right then. Marlene was a pimp. At first I thought she was a prostitute, but then one night she told me she had a few girls who were street-walkers and who obtained customers. She told me they arrested her for being a pimp and that she thought it was unfair because she considered her girls as her children . . ."

"And you believed that, Mitzi?"

"Of course not! Don't be silly! I may be a simple teacher who hasn't seen much of the world, but I don't fall for a story like that one! I told her she was lying and that the relationships between her and her girls must be a totally commercial one."

"And what did she say?"

"She smiled."

"That was all?"

Mitzi nodded.

"Within a few days I knew Marlene was one of the greatest liars I had met. I told her so and again she smiled. She didn't contradict me. As a matter of fact she didn't say anything at all."

"Nevertheless you liked her, didn't you?"

Mitzi nodded slowly and there was a puzzled look in her eyes.

"Yes, I did. And honestly, doctor . . . that is something I really don't understand. I did know who and what she was and yet . . ."

"Yet you loved her?"

"Yes . . . I mean, no . . . No, not at the beginning. It took some time . . . After a few days I started getting to know her. I felt she was interested in me and that gave me a strange satisfaction. At night we talked. She told me of her youth and of her family . . . She had a wonderful sense of humour and pretty soon I liked her. Then, suddenly, I discovered I was in love with her."

139

"Did you think that strange? After all you were engaged to be married."

She thought a few moments and then shook her head.

"No . . . No, I didn't think that was strange . . . I thought it wonderful . . . It was wonderful to know that there in that grey building was someone who cared for me . . . who loved me too. I realised it was different from the love I felt for Paul. Suddenly Paul seemed very, very far away."

"When he came to visit you, you didn't tell him of your feelings?"

"Of course not! "

"Why not?"

She hesitated.

"I . . . I was afraid he wouldn't understand. Besides I thought it was something that would pass . . ."

"And did it pass?"

Slowly she shook her head.

"No, it didn't, doctor. My love for Marlene grew . . . became more intense . . . As a matter of fact it frightened me, but I could not resist . . . You know, Marlene was only a few years older than I and very beautiful. She had this shock of black hair and green eyes—kind of dreamy, I think—that fascinated me. She wasn't very talkative. Sometimes she spoke about herself, but most of the time I did the talking and she just listened. She was a wonderful listener . . . I felt that everything I told her really interested her. She absorbed my words, stimulated me . . . and all the time she kept looking at me with those strange green eyes of hers . . . Afterwards, when it had happened, I wondered if maybe she had hypnotised me . . ."

"Tell me exactly what happened, Mitzi."

"It was a few days before Christmas. Paul had come to visit me and after he had left, I felt depressed. I don't know why. It was just a feeling . . . That night Marlene and I were in our cell. I talked about Christmas when I had been a child and she said that each year she bought

140

presents for what she called 'her girls'. I didn't believe her and told her so. 'You're a liar, Marlene,' I said. She just looked at me and smiled and said softly: 'You think so, Mitzi?' We sat on my bed, our bodies touching. I had the feeling her eyes looked at me all the time. I laughed and said I really thought so. Then I looked at her and suddenly I had a strange, haunted feeling . . . As if I was going to drown in those two eyes, those eyes that kept looking at me and seemed to change slowly into a green lake in which I sank . . ." Mitzi was silent for a few moments. I knew her thoughts were far away. There was a dreamy, strangely longing look in her eyes, as if she tried to re-live those moments.

'Then what happened, Mitzi?" I asked softly.

"I . . . I don't know . . ." She shook her head. "Suddenly she held me in her arms and we were kissing . . . I felt her hands on my body . . . caressing . . . fondling . . . We made love to each other . . . She taught me techniques I had never known . . . After about an hour we went to sleep in each other's arms . . . It was heaven, doctor . . . It was the greatest thing that had ever happened in my life. Next morning, when I awoke, I knew that I had never loved a man or woman as I loved Marlene . . ."

I asked Mitzi how they made love and she told me it happened by mutual masturbation.

"I guess all the inmates did it that way," she said reflectively. "They must have known what had happened, for after that night they called us lovers . . ."

"Did the matrons know?"

"Yes, they did. Don't forget the grapevine in a prison works fast and very thoroughly . . . I felt they knew . . . One or two were jealous—almost every one of them was a lesbian, you know—and it was said that Marlene was going to be deprived of her special privileges, but that never happened."

That was the beginning of an affair that changed Mitzi's entire life. When her sentence was finished, Marlene had to

141

stay in prison for another three months. When Mitzi said goodbye, she promised her lover to wait for her. As soon as she left prison she broke her engagement with Paul, telling him that her sentence had given her time to think and that she knew now that she did not love him enough to marry him.

"He was heartbroken, but accepted the situation. I think he really loved me . . . I don't think he knew what was the real reason I broke the engagement. It was pathetic . . ."

Mitzi moved to the city where Marlene lived and rented there an apartment. She took a job at an office and waited till her lover would come back. Then, three months later, the day came and the two were united again.

"I'll never forget the moment I opened the door and saw her standing before me . . . I cried . . . Marlene couldn't speak a word either. She just looked at me with those strange green eyes of hers . . . Then something seemed to snap inside my head . . . I took her in my arms . . . We embraced and cried . . . Oh, I don't think I've ever been that happy in my life . . . I felt I should never be unhappy again . . . Of course that was a mistake . . ."

She was silent and shook her head. I waited patiently, but Mitzi did not continue.

"What happened, Mitzi?" I asked. "What happened that shattered that dream of happiness?"

She shrugged.

"I . . . I don't know . . . Or maybe I do know . . . Anyhow I don't know whose fault it was . . . Look here, doctor. After all I was a small-town schoolmistress . . . I mean my standards were different from Marlene's . . . Maybe that was my fault . . . I should have known that to her life wasn't a rosy-coloured love-affair . . ."

"What do you mean, Mitzi?"

Absentmindedly she ran her fingers through her fair, long hair.

"Marlene wanted me to be in business with her . . . I mean as a partner . . . Only—she wanted to be the pimp

142

and I had to be the street-girl . . . She promised me half of our income. She would give all her other girls the sack. From that moment it was going to be just her and me . . . I think she meant it . . . She . . . she really loved me I suppose . . ."

"What did you do? What was your reaction?"

She smiled sadly.

"I was shocked. I told her to go to hell and made it clear I'd never do a thing like that. Well, it was my up-bringing I suppose, that made me say things like that. Poor Marlene didn't understand. I had wounded her feelings . . . I think she was very sincere when she made me that proposition . . ." Again she smiled. "Poor Marlene . . ."

"Then what happened. You had a row, I suppose?"

"Yes, we had a row. All kinds of unpleasant things were said by both of us and at the end we parted. I left her the apartment and went back to my home-town . . . With some trouble I succeeded in getting back my job as a teacher. Somebody told me Paul had left for a distant town and wasn't coming back. Well, I worked and worked and tried to forget what had happened."

I looked at her reflectively and said:

"But you couldn't forget and that's the reason you're here to ask my advice."

"That's right, doctor. All this happened about a year ago. Since then I have tried in every way to forget Marlene . . . I tried to find men that interested me . . . I joined a few clubs, took a holiday . . . There isn't a thing I didn't try to put her out of my mind. But it didn't work . . ." She smiled sadly and apologetically. "There isn't a day that I do not think of Marlene . . . You must help me, doctor. I can't get on like this. I'm afraid I'll go out of my mind . . ."

"There's one important question we have to answer first," I said. "Why does Marlene mean so much to you?"

"Because I love her!" She looked surprised.

143

"That's not what I mean. Why do you love her? Why does she attract you? Why are you, as you call it, fascinated by her?"

It was clear Mitzi had never tried to answer these questions herself. As a matter of fact I didn't think she had ever asked them. Up till now she had taken her love for Marlene for granted.

In the weeks that followed, I tried to collect enough information to get a clear picture of her childhood. She told me about her parents—details, I think, she must have told Marlene during the long and lonely nights in their cell—and slowly, very slowly before my mind's eye arose the image of a pitiable love-starved child. Her father was a very shy and submissive man. Her mother was a very extrovert woman, who was always busy outside the home and on the whole cared little for family life, her husband and her only child.

When her father died, Mitzi was twelve years old. Her mother was very seldom at home and hired a woman to look after her daughter. Mitzi never liked the woman and as she grew older she felt more and more lonely.

I soon discovered that her love for Marlene was—as is often the case with lesbians—only a love for a mother-substitute. She loved Marlene because this friend gave her the love Mitzi's mother lacked. Suddenly I remembered what she had told me: "I don't think my mother ever cared for me like Marlene did." I realised these words were the key to her love.

I told her my conclusion. Mitzi thought about it and then nodded.

"I think you're right, doctor. Marlene was something like a mother to me . . ."

"If you want to forget her, you'll have to realise that you're a grown-up now and that you need no longer a mother who loves you and cares for you. It is sad your mother didn't love you when you were a child, but that is a long time ago . . . You'll have to be conscious of the

144

fact that the motive of your love for Marlene is very simple: you love her because she loved you as your mother didn't love you when you were young."

Again she nodded.

"I see what you mean, doctor . . ."

We talked about her childhood. After a few more visits Mitzi broke off the treatment. I tried to contact her, but in vain. A neighbour told me she had moved. A few months later I heard from her again. She wrote me a letter to thank me for my trouble.

"It isn't your fault, doctor," she wrote, "but I didn't think it wise to resist any longer the orders my heart gave me. I've gone back to Marlene. Your small-town schoolmistress no longer teaches, but solicits customers for her pimp. Oh, I know you'll be shocked, but I don't care. Marlene did gave her other girls the sack and now we both have a partnership. We live again in the same apartment and I'm very happy. I don't know if this relationship of ours will last, but I keep my fingers crossed. Sometimes we talk of the day we met in that cell. We both know now that it was a lucky day that changed our lives."

Mitzi's case-history brings to my mind a letter written by a girl, who was about to leave the reformatory, to her friend who was still an inmate. It was published by Frank S. Caprio in his book about lesbianism.[3] It speaks of the same sincere feelings of love that made Mitzi go back to Marlene, her lover with the green eyes:

" . . . I do love you and God only knows how much. I could never play games with you, because for the first time in my life I think I could be happy. I never went too much for women before you came along, but now I'll never be any good without one, and that one has to be you. I won't promise you anything, because I know you won't believe me, so I'll prove myself first, and then do you think you could care enough to come out in the free world and be with me?"

Many lesbian women and many women with latent

145

homosexual tendencies found in a relationship, that started
in prison, a lasting happiness. Maybe this is one of the
positive points of the problem homosexuality in the prison
undoubtedly is.

AN ARMY OF AMAZONS

There are legends about armies of warlike women that
conquered countries, defeated male adversaries and turned
them into slaves. The Amazons were the most glorious of
them, as indicated in our historical survey.

The word "Amazon" is Greek and means "those without breasts". The Amazons were a very warlike tribe
consisting exclusively of women, supposedly living at
the Thermodon river in Kappadocia. Their queen was
Hyppolitha and according to Greek mythology she married Theseus.[4] From Kappadocia the Amazons moved
to the east coast of the Black Sea.

Of course it is tempting to compare lesbians who serve
in the army, navy and air-force women's corps with these
legendary Amazons. However, according to most historians the Amazons never really existed, as mentioned
before. Probably the ancient Greeks knew something about
some Asian tribes where women had gained supremacy
and this knowledge developed into the story of the Amazons about which Homer wrote.

A certain type of lesbian always has been interested in
the army and army life. She followed the Amazons'
example and enlisted and even went to war because she
was attracted by this pre-eminently masculine activity.
Other lesbians—the ones attracted by masculine females
—enlisted in the armies because they knew this to be an
opportunity to meet other lesbians.

In World War I at the Russian front lots of Austrian and
Russian prisoners of war, after internment, turned out
to be women in disguise, and on the battlefields were

146

found dead soldiers who appeared to be not men at all. Hirschfeld[5] cites some very interesting cases of lesbians who went to war and behaved and fought as men. After discovery of their true identity the fate of these captured women in travesty often was horrifying. Hirschfeld publishes a ghastly picture of a killed Russian soldier who proved to be a woman. After she was made a prisoner of war by the Austrians and it was discovered that she was not a male, she was tortured and raped by a great number of soldiers and afterwards shot. The body was left in a roadside ditch.

One of the most famous women who fought in the First World War as a soldier, was the Austrian Martha Liebeneiner. She had fought two years in the trenches, next to unsuspecting men, before she was seriously wounded and it turned out that this brave soldier was not male but female! The astonishing thing was that Martha—who really looked and acted as a man—had a certain fame as a woman-chaser.

She was a regular visitor to an army-brothel and was regarded by her comrades as a connoisseur on the subject of women. After the true story about Martha became known, it appeared that one of the inmates of the brothel knew that Martha was a woman. Both women were lesbians and had started a relationship. After her recovery Martha was sent to the Fatherland. About three months later she tried anew to enlist, but was not accepted as her old injuries made her "unfit for military service". Due to her cunning conduct during a—very superficial—medical examination it seems nobody suspected her to be a woman.

A striking phenomenon of World War II was that almost no cases of women fighting in disguise are known. Of course the very strict medical examination to which soldiers were subjected made it impossible for lesbians to smuggle themselves into an army of men. However, there was also a second reason. Almost every participating country had its own women's corps and it is a well-known fact that these women's corps were a real "home for lesbians". According to Donald Webster Cory⁶ a lesbian who served in the United States Army as a WAC told him: "About 70 per cent of the girls in my camp were gay—70 per cent." The same girl gave a remarkable explanation of the advantages of such a great percentage of female homosexuals:

"There wouldn't be a Women's Army Corps without the gay girls. (. . .) They're the solid, tough group that keeps the companies together. You find them everywhere— officers, enlisted women, non-coms—getting along with the straight girls, minding their own business, getting work done, and never getting pregnant. Pregnancy—do you know pregnancy is the biggest single problem that the WACs face! Thousands of girls get discharged for being pregnant. With all the pregnancies, if it wasn't for the gay girls, these companies would fall apart at the seams."

It is not only in the women's corps of the armies, navies and air-forces of the Western world that great numbers of lesbians can be found, but also in the female sections of the police forces. Very often both partners of a "couple" work in the same unit. Here—as in prisons—lesbians give each other names such as "mother", "daddy", "brother", "sister", "auntie" and "uncle". This is not as strange as it may seem. Most lesbians had a very unhappy family life when they were children and in playing the parts of "mother", "brother," "auntie" or "sister" they only stage a rather tragic comedy. They try to establish the family life they so pathetically lacked in their childhood.

When I first heard about this strange make-believe I smiled. Then Ursula, a girl who was a lesbian and worked for some time as a female police officer, told me of the seriousness with which the girls played their parts.

"They really try hard to get the feeling they are related to each other," she said. "I've known an 'auntie' who spent all her money to pay the bills of the girl she called her 'niece' when this girl was in hospital. . . . Only when you

148

yourself have seen the jealousy that arises when a girl makes passes at another one she isn't 'related' to, you'll understand this is not just a game to kill time. It is a very serious attempt to establish a kind of family—the kind of family most of these girls have never known in reality . . ."

"What happens to a girl that is a newcomer?" I asked.

"When she is straight nothing happens. Only if it turns out she is a lesbian, she is 'adopted' by a 'daddy' and accepted in the group. They never let each other down . . . I've seen lesbian 'couples' who had been together for ten years or more and who even wore wedding rings . . .'

Male homosexuals have a preference for certain professions. The feminine type of male homosexual likes to work as a fashion designer, a window dresser, a ballet dancer or hairdresser. The masculine type sometimes is sailor, truck driver or boxer. The public almost never realises there exists such a thing as a male homosexual who is very masculine in appearance and makes an impression of potency. The feminine "gay boys" are the ones that attract attention.

Likewise the public thinks all lesbians are masculine in appearance and work as prisons matrons, female policemen or are in military service. As it is with the feminine-mannered male homosexual, the masculine lesbian, "the butch", draws all the attention.

Maybe it is useful to state once again that most homosexuals—male and female—are ordinary looking people who do not act suspiciously in any way. It is just plain nonsense to assume that one "always easily can spot a homosexual." Of course there is a certain group of homosexuals that would even draw attention from a blind man, but this is a minority. Ursula once told me of a non-homosexual friend of hers who told her she could very easily spot a lesbian. Once they walked through the shopping-centre of the town and at the end of the walk the friend said proudly she had seen at least thirty-three women who were lesbians.

149

"Oh! I wish you would tell me how you spot them!" Ursula said.

The friend shook her head and smiled.

"I'm afraid I can't tell you," she said. "You know, it is a kind of instinct that tells me. . . . You would never be able to learn to do it. . . . I'm sure you know nothing of these things!" That friend never suspected Ursula of being a lesbian and I think this indicates how erroneous is the popular belief that "it isn't very difficult to spot a homosexual".

NOTES

1. Joan Henry: *Women in Prison*, New York 1952.

2. Joseph Fishman, former inspector of federal prisons, quoted by Frank S. Caprio.

3. Frank S. Caprio: *Female Homosexuality a Psychodynamic Study of Lesbianism*, New York 1954, London 1957.

4. For more about this mythological marriage see Mary Renault: *The King Must Die*, New York 1958.

5. Magnus Hirschfeld: *Sittengeschichte des Weltkrieges*, Leipzig 1926.

6. Donald Webster Cory: *The Lesbian in America*, New York 1964.

CHAPTER TEN

Man and Lesbian Love

This chapter deals with men—an exception in a book about lesbian love. In the following pages we pay attention to the fact that very many heterosexual men are sexually stimulated by witnessing lesbian love-making and we shall try to expose the motives of their interest.

All prostitutes know about the interest some men have in lesbian love-play. The plushy brothels of the world's capitals treat their customers to the "Grand Spectacle"—in American bawdy-houses it is named "Circus"—that is an extensive orgy of lesbian love-play. In many cities street-walkers operate in pairs. The customer who asks for "lesbian specialities" is taken to a room where he can feast his eyes upon the sex-show the duo presents for his sake. Big-city prostitutes who operate alone get reinforcements from fellow-prostitutes if a customer wants sex with a lesbian slant.

The visitor to a bawdy-house who wants to see lesbians at work, and the artist who specialises in depicting lesbian love-play clearly have something in common: a profound interest about homosexual love-making.

Why does the visitor not ask for an orgy with homosexual males as participants? Why does the artist not depict the intimate details of male homosexuality? The answer is: because both are repelled by it.

No man and no woman is exclusively heterosexual. In all of us homosexual and heterosexual components are

151

mingled up to a certain point. When the homosexual components dominate, the man or woman is a straight homosexual. Another possibility is that the individual is heterosexual, but that the homosexual components are strong enough to make themselves known and to disturb him.

If a man is conscious of his homosexual side he can learn to live with it. Alas, most individuals prefer to repress these feelings and to deny them. Naturally this is no solution at all. The homosexual components do not disappear but start looking for another outlet. Of course these individuals feel an exaggerated horror for anything that has to do with male homosexuality and consider it a threat to their virtue. By the way, to this group of individuals belong the men who are forever demanding that the authorities take measures against the "ever-growing homosexual threat to our civilisation".

As these men have barred themselves the way to a straight homosexual outlet, they can only—unconsciously —enjoy the pleasures of homosexuality by way of a detour.

Psychoanalysts agree about the fact that men who are sexually stimulated by watching two lesbians making love to each other, have strong homosexual tendencies of which they are not conscious. While watching lesbian love-making they identify themselves unconsciously with one of the lovers, and consequently the realisation that they are participating in homosexual acts stimulates them. If it was not for this realisation they would not be interested in lesbianism at all, as it is much easier for a heterosexual to identify himself with a man making love to a woman than to see himself a woman loving another one.

To most of the men who like to watch lesbians making love and regard this interest as a "refined speciality" of heterosexual love-life, this will come as a shock. Homosexual components most of the time are so ruthlessly repressed by the individual, that not the faintest notion exists

152

that all this could have something to do with homosexuality. Men who do not have the opportunity of watching lesbian love-making take to masturbation while imagining scenes of debaucheries between female homosexuals. A curious fact is, that straight male homosexuals do not show any interest in lesbian love-play.

THE PHOTOGRAPHS A PATIENT COLLECTED

Sometimes this interest in lesbians and consequently the identification with them can take very strange shapes.

One of my pre-war patients was a bachelor of 43 we will name Hans. He was a prosperous man and lived with several servants in a big house in the centre of town. He came to ask me for advice on his insomnia and during the interviews that followed I learned some details about his love-life.

Though Hans was rich and had enough money to satisfy all his sexual desires, he preferred what he used to call "solo-sex"—masturbation supported by imagined scenes of sexual happenings between lesbians.

"Why lesbians?" I asked.

He shrugged.

"I don't know. It always has been that way."

"Why don't you look for a pair of real life lesbians? And if you're not able to find them, why don't you go to a brothel and state your wishes? Surely they will be able to help you there!'

Hans refused to be drawn. He mumbled something about being too shy to speak to women and about it always having been this way.

I tried again.

"Surely it must be very tiring to imagine time and time again the same scenes!"

He shook his head.

153

"No . . ." He smiled embarrassedly. "I . . . I've got my little assistants, you know."

I looked at him curiously.

"You've your little . . . what?"

"My assistants . . . Oh, you won't understand . . ."

I knew this was important. His answer didn't discourage me. As I was sure his insomnia had something to do with his sex-life I just had to know the workings of his imagination.

I told Hans that I only could help him if he trusted me completely and held no information back.

"Oh, I think you're right," he said pensively. "But don't think it's easy to lay bare the most intimate details of your life . . ."

I nodded.

"All right. Back to your little assistants. Who are they?"

He shrugged.

"You'll think me silly if you hear . . ." He didn't finish that sentence, but looked at me steadily and said: "All right. I'll tell you everything."

It appeared my patient had a tremendous collection of pornographic pictures. As he was often abroad he had suppliers in almost all countries of Western Europe. He spent the evenings of his bachelor existence with the arranging, describing and filing of his pictures. He masturbated regularly and then focussed his attention on a number of pictures he chose beforehand. The women that figured in his pornographic photographs he called his "little assistants".

One day Hans showed me a part of his collection. It existed of original photographs and on all of them women were pictured in lewd positions and participating in lesbian activities.

"Are all your photographs like these?" I asked.

He looked at me and I saw he did not understand me.

"I mean . . . Are they all pictures of lesbians?"

He nodded.

"That's right . . . I've a special interest in lesbians, you know."

"And in that tremendous collection of yours there isn't *one* picture of a normal coition?"

He shook his head and smiled.

"Do you think that abnormal, doctor?"

"Do you?"

Again he shrugged.

"Maybe yes. Maybe no. Who is to say what's normal?"

I looked at the photographs that lay before me on my desk. They were glossy enlargements of professionally taken photographs. The lighting was well done and the scenes were photographed from an angle that made the best of the very lewd situations that were pictured. All sexual variations between lesbians were practised. There were pictures of cunnilingus, mutual masturbation, anilingus and flagellation scenes. On a great number of photographs a false penis was used and this gave the opportunity to picture pseudo-fellatio, pseudo-coition and pederastic scenes.

"Did you buy all these pictures?" I asked.

"No, not all of them," Hans said. He looked at me proudly. "You know, doctor, I'm a pretty good photographer myself. I've a dark-room where I can develop and print my films and I make the enlargements myself. Of course the greatest part of my collection I've bought. I know dealers in Brussels, Stockholm, Paris, Copenhagen, Amsterdam and Münich . . . These men know exactly what I want and they are ever on the lookout for photographs they know they can sell to me. I must admit it has cost me an awful lot of money but you can be sure this is the greatest collection of its kind in the entire world. I put years and years of my life into it."

I looked at the photographs and thought of the thousands of others he had at home. "It is a very remarkable collection, to say the least," I ventured.

"Good!" He looked as happy as a child.

"Hans . . ." Again I looked at the photographs. "Tell

155

me, where did you find the girls that posed for these pictures? Were they real lesbians?"

"I prefer to think they were." He looked uneasy as if he did not want to doubt the sexual interests of his models. "As a matter of fact they were not difficult to find. Some of them are prostitutes I paid. The others are girls who call themselves models. There are models in some cities who are willing to pose for every kind of picture. Some of them have their own studios and photographic equipment. That's where I made these pictures. If more girls were needed— as you see some photographs picture scenes of lesbian orgies—they brought their friends in. Well, I had to pay them a stiff sum of money, but I think these pictures are unique . . . Even my dealer in Münich hadn't ever seen photographs like these. And yet he's well known in the trade because of the exclusivity of his photographs!"

Hans talked about his amazing collection of pornography with the pride and knowledge of an owner of a valuable stamp collection.

"Do you have a friend who knows of the existence of this collection?" I asked.

He shook his head.

"No. I wouldn't like it if there was somebody who knew. Don't think I'm ashamed!" he continued hurriedly. "It's just that I wouldn't want . . . to share it with somebody else. They're mine!"

"What do you mean?" I asked quietly. "The photographs or the women that are pictured?"

For a few moments he looked at me silently. Then, very slowly, he said:

"Both of them."

I soon discovered that Hans was in love with some of the girls that posed for the photographs. Some of these models he had met when they posed for him. Others figured in photographs he had bought abroad and he had never met them.

156

"These girls you photographed yourself, did they know you were in love with them?"

"Of course not!" He looked at me indignantly. "I hardly spoke to them on the occasion. Later, when the photographs were developed and enlarged I fell in love with them. As soon as that happened I took care not to meet the girl any more. I was afraid I'd be disappointed if I saw her again. I just looked for another model."

"So you just loved the pictures of your favourites?"

He shook his head.

"No, you can't say that, doctor. You can't put it as easily as that."

"Why not?"

He smiled in an embarrassed way.

"To me . . . they all are alive. I mean . . . My imagination makes them alive. They move and talk and do whatever I want."

"I see." I looked at him. Hans was not deformed or ugly, yet it was clear that he was afraid of women. Why? I talked with him and discovered he was afraid women would not take him seriously.

"I'm always afraid they would just laugh at me if I'd make passes," he said, shaking his head.

After a few interviews it was clear to me that Hans was homosexual, but did not suspect it himself. He just told himself he was satisfied with his "solo-sex" and his "little assistants" and was not interested at all in real women. Why was he interested in pictures of lesbian debaucheries? He never tried to answer that question.

I told him the motive that started his amazing collection.

"You're an individual with very strong homosexual tendencies, Hans. Only you won't admit it to yourself and so the homosexual interests in you have to make a detour to find satisfaction. They are at the base of your taste for lesbian scenes. You're interested and stimulated by your collection of photographs because every picture gives you

157

the opportunity to identify yourself unconsciously with one of the lesbian lovers and so to taste those homosexual pleasures you have denied yourself."

Thunderstruck he looked at me.

"But I don't understand, doctor . . . I mean . . . I never felt attracted to men . . ."

"Of course not! If you had, your homosexuality would have come into the open and this is exactly the thing you did not want to happen because your moral standards did not permit you to be one. That is the reason why you had to invent a substitute. It is evident that your interest in lesbians making love has become this substitute."

"But . . . but why do you think I'm . . ." He couldn't force himself to pronounce the word.

"That you have strong homosexual tendencies is clear to me, Hans," I said. "What's the cause of it—that's something we are going to find out."

A few more sessions gave me a clear picture of some important events in Hans's childhood.

He had always been a rather shy boy. He had only a few friends and most of the time he was on his own. He did not mind. Hans as a boy liked being alone and as he was an ardent reader he never felt bored. He never showed much interest in his surroundings and consequently still was not interested in girls when he was twelve. At that age, however, something happened that had an important influence on the further course of his life.

While walking through his neighbourhood Hans became mixed up in a quarrel between several small children. He tried to mediate but without success. Suddenly the older sister of one of the children appeared and mistook Hans to be the instigator of the quarrel. She was a big girl of about twenty years of age and made short work of the "warmonger". She put him over her knee and gave him a good thrashing. Then she let him go.

This incident meant that Hans lost all his trust in women. When he grew up he got more and more the impression

158

they never would take him seriously and he became scared of them. These feelings developed his homosexual tendencies. As he unconsciously censored these homosexual feelings he focussed his interest on homosexual women instead of on homosexual men.

As soon as Hans realised this, his insomnia gradually disappeared. This surprised him, but I told him his insomnia had been the consequence of his unconscious resistance against his psychic build-up.

A prolonged treatment had the result that Hans got rid of his collection and for the first time in his life started getting interested in living, normal girls.

A SIGNIFICANT TEST

Psychoanalysts have made the male interest in lesbian love a subject of research. Dettmann[1] tested a number of men by showing them three pictures of two lesbians and wrote down their reactions. The pictures were clipped from a Japanese erotic magazine. They were definitely not obscene but significant enough to give the interviewed persons an opportunity to draw their conclusions.

The first of the pictures showed two Japanese women, dressed only in a bra and a slip, embracing. The second picture showed them engaged in passionate kissing. In the third picture one of them was trussed up and gagged by the other.

The reactions these photographs drew forth made it clear that feminine men in particular showed interest. They spoke of the masculine character of the pictured females and proved again the rule that the interest a man shows for masculinity in a woman is commensurate with the feminine tendencies in his own character. One of the interviewed men, though married, had known homoerotic experiences. Of the masculine men who showed interest some reactions clearly showed disappointment with their own masculine sex and the desire to play the part of a woman in lesbian love-making.

Dettmann concludes that male interest in lesbian love consists sometimes of sado-masochistic and voyeuristic tendencies, but that the factor of homosexual components in a man is the most important cause of his interest in this regard. In an explanation of his test Dettmann illustrates his theories with a very interesting case-history of a forty-five-year-old working man, married, with two children. His interest in lesbian love-making made him write—just for the pleasure he got out of it—a number of "novels" with a lesbian theme. These novels were kept in a drawer and the author never showed them to anybody. The descriptions of love-play between two girls—both inmates of a boarding-school for girls—make clear the interests of the writer. The following fragment is a description of love-play between Gisela and Ingrid. Gisela unconsciously is in love with one of her teachers, a Miss Schattenschneider. The fragment opens with Gisela crying because her beloved Miss Schattenschneider gave her a (flagellantic) thrashing:

Gisela couldn't stop crying. Moonlight lightened her lovely face and made the tears at her cheeks glitter like pearls. Ingrid, who was lying in the bed next to her, couldn't look at it any more. Up to this moment she never felt much sympathy for Gisela. Ingrid's character was totally different. She was a dare-devil in gymnastics, troublesome during lessons and always the cock of the walk among her friends. Many times she had laughed at sentimental girls like Gisela. She thought it silly that Gisela felt sympathy for the geometry teacher she herself thought a beast. This afternoon she had heard how Miss Schattenschneider had flogged poor Gisela and now she knew exactly what the poor girl, who was lying next to her, felt.

Was it wise to talk to the crying girl? Gisela in her

160

distress seemed to have hidden herself behind an invisible wall.

"Gisela!" Ingrid cried softly.

The crying girl didn't hear it.

Ingrid sat up in her bed. She looked around her and listened. All the other girls slept. Ingrid left her bed and still nobody saw what she was doing. Sitting at her bed Ingrid touched the trembling face of the crying girl. The girl next to her was shocked and asked unwillingly: "What do you want?"

"Everything isn't as bad as that," Ingrid said. "I don't think Miss Schattenschneider really wanted to harm you."

"Leave me alone," Gisela said. This time her voice didn't sound as cool as the first time and she wasn't crying any longer.

Now Ingrid sat down on the bed of the other girl. The moon made her night-gown look white as snow.

"All this will pass," she said. "Soon we'll be grown-up. Then we'll leave this school. We'll live a life of our own and we'll find a man who will love us . . ."

"I don't want to know any men!" Gisela interrupted. "No man would be worthy to reach Miss Schattenschneider a glass of water! She is wise . . . so energetic . . ."

"But isn't that exactly the reason why you're crying?" Ingrid asked. "Nevertheless I think you're right. In gymnastics I'm much better than many boys and still they speak of us as the weaker sex! It's not fair the way they look down upon us women."

"No one would look down upon you!" Gisela said with a certainty that surprised Ingrid. She had never suspected that this girl admired her because of her robustness. Now she, on the other hand, felt admiration for Gisela because this girl was so different. This discovery made her blush. Before she knew what was happening she bent over Gisela and pressed a kiss on her cheek.

161

"Oh! Do you really like me?" Gisela asked, full of hope. The only answer Ingrid could give was lying down next to Gisela. It was the right answer at the right moment, for Gisela pushed away her blankets and said softly: "Come . . ." and then the blankets closed down upon a new friendship.

"Sometimes it's good to be sad," Gisela said after a long silence. "When you're very sad and then something wonderful happens, you're able to feel better how happy you are."

"Life is just a long row of ups and downs," Ingrid said with a wisdom she had never suspected she possessed. "If it was different, life wouldn't be what it is now!"

"Ssst!" Gisela said suddenly. Hannah, a girl that slept in a bed on the other side of her, had moved. She mumbled something, but it was only a dream that made her do it and she didn't wake up.

"Strange, that no one suspects what lives in the hearts of other people," Gisela said softly.

"Let's not say another word," Ingrid said. "It is much nicer that way."

She pressed her young body closer to the body of her newly found friend and felt through the thin material of the night-gown the warmth of the other girl. Silently she put her arm around the neck of her friend.

Time passed slowly like sand in an hour-glass. After an eternity of silence, Gisela whispered: "What strong muscles you have!" Her hands touched Ingrid's arms and legs.

"And you're so soft," the other girl said as quietly. Ingrid's hand touched Gisela's girlish breasts. The playful fingers made the nipples erect. "You're a real woman already . . ."

"And the . . . the other thing . . . I've had too!" said Gisela proudly. She couldn't think of a way to put it more clearly.

Yet Ingrid had understood what she meant.

162

"Oh, but I'm almost a year younger!" she said apologetically. It belonged to the mysteries she had told herself about of which she wasn't curious. This time however, she wondered what it meant to go through it for the first time.

She caressed Gisela's legs. Her movements made the night-gown move higher up. At the same time she looked a bit scared at Gisela's face. There was no trace of resistance, but only surrender—as if she dreamed with her eyes wide open.

Gisela breathed heavily. Her eyes seemed blind. She had put her left arm around Ingrid's neck. Her right hand was magnetically attracted to Ingrid's breasts. The two hemispheres were still small and yet they gave her a feeling of happiness she had never known. The breasts of Miss Schattenschneider were also very small she thought. Dreams of another embrace existed for only one heartbeat and then disappeared. Only Ingrid was real.

The warmth of the girl's body. The sound of her breathing, mingling with the sound of her own breath. The beating of the two hearts. The touch of Ingrid's almost childish breasts under her fingers. Ingrid's caresses, deep down her body—this was a new reality. It was like penetrating into a new, fascinating world.

Gisela felt it as an alarm, that sounded through her body, through all her limbs and nerves, awoke her emotions and whipped up her passions.

She couldn't lie still any longer. The accumulation of her passions forced her into wild movements. Now there was no more reality. Nothing was left now—no dormitory, no bed, no moon. Even Ingrid and she herself disappeared. And after that again nothing, a totally different nothingness: full of sweet rest.

"Well, did you like it?" asked an unpleasant voice in the bed next to hers. "You dirty little pigs! Imagine what would happen if I told Miss Schattenschneider what you have done! Oh, don't you worry . . . I wouldn't

163

care if somebody did the same thing to me . . . Only I'm
not a novice like the two of you! "

So Hannah hadn't slept after all! She had seen everything and heard everything . . . Hannah—of all people!
This little beast of a girl! Now all happiness was pulled
down into the mud . . .

As the author of these and other fragments wrote them
only for his own pleasure and kept his "novels" carefully
hidden, it is clear that writing them, as Dettmann observes,
was a kind of fetishism.

"While I'm writing I feel wonderful . . . I've lost touch
with reality . . . Only when I'm finished I come down to
earth," he admitted. These words remind one of the en-
thusiastic descriptions fetishists give of the emotions that
well up in them while handling their fetishes. Writing his
novels gave this amateur author a "spiritual orgasm".

Psychoanalysts know very well the phenomenon of the
"Satan's Bible". One could easily call it the "fetishist's
handbook". Most fetishists are in the habit of clipping
pictures from magazines that have a relation to their fetish.
These pictures are pasted into an album and supplied with
a text. Most of the times the fetishist in his "Satan's Bible"
writes down a fantasy that is characteristic for his kind of
fetishism and illustrates his story with the pictures he
chooses.

Active flagellants—who combine sado-masochism and
nates-fetishism in one person—cherish a true prediliction
for "Satan's Bibles". Such an album is a great help for
the psychoanalyst if he wants to analyse the sexual interests
of a patient.

The amateur author who wrote down the touching story
of Gisela and Ingrid made no use of clippings from magazines to find inspiration and to illustrate his "novel".
Nevertheless Dettmann states these "novels" were the most
important "Satan's Bibles" he ever set eyes on.

Next to homosexuality, sado-masochism is a widespread

sexual variation. We know now that every human being has more or less homosexual tendencies. It is the same with sado-masochism. Every man and every woman has sado-masochistic tendencies that help decide his or her character. Of course homosexuals have also sado-masochistic components and the mixture of homosexuality and sado-masochism can have striking results. In the next chapter we will take a closer view at the sado-masochistic homosexual.

The subject is an important one as "masochistic provocation and injustice-collecting" (Bergler[2]) is one of the elements of which the personality of a homosexual—both male and female—consists.

NOTES

1. Kurt Dettmann: *Der Mann und die Lesbische Liebe*, Hamburg 1963.

2. Edmund Bergler: *Homosexuality, Disease or Way of Life?*, New York 1956.

CHAPTER ELEVEN

Sadistic Lesbians and Willing Victims

In the United States "Bondage-magazines" are very much in demand. Among curious American publications that have reached Continental shores the "bondage-magazines" have an important place: at the news-stands and in the hearts of the bondage-fans.

The greater part of these remarkable magazines consists of photographs of 'women in bondage''. Not only these magazines, their illustrations also look alike. In every picture two women figure: one is being bound, gagged, kicked or flogged by the other. Both women are mostly dressed only in slip and bra and most of the scenes are photographed in a typical American living-room. A man not interested in this kind of publication can easily say: "If you've seen one, you've seen them all."

Not thus the bondage-fan.

To him every pose and every picture is different in an exciting way. The length of the ropes, the position of the victim, the knot made by the "mistress"—they are all important to him. The most subtle variation of a scene gives him new pleasure.

Sociologists consider the bondage-craze that is sweeping the United States, as a refined revenge of the American male on the American female and her "momism"[1] that has turned the American society with its powerful women's clubs into a matriarchy. The American male, helpless at the mercy of the "deadliest of the species", projects his resist-

166

ance and discomfort on bondage-scenes in which women are tortured, flogged and gagged.

But why are these actions performed by women? Why are these female victims the bondage-magazines depict, not beaten, kicked and tied up by men?

The sociologists have an answer to that.

"If men were going to figure in these photographs," they explain, "the censor would prohibit these magazines for being lewd. As long as the magazines have an all-female cast nobody will think of calling them obscene. The phenomenon of total absence of men is just a gimmick of the publishers to prevent prosecution by the law."

This sounds a reasonable argument and yet I think there is another reason for these "all-girl orchestras" that figure in the bondage-magazines. It is not only for the sake of decency that men are excluded from the pages.

In lesbian love flagellation is a well-known phenomenon —not less than it is in heterosexual love-life. Many famous artists depicted flagellation scenes with a lesbian slant. This predilection can as well express itself in a sweet and lovely "flagellation game" at a boarding-school for girls as in the most cruel actions.

It is this flagellation among lesbians that is depicted in the bondage-magazines. It is significant that one of the pictures Dettmann showed to the men he used for his test, was such a picture from a Japanese bondage-magazine.

What is the background of mutual flagellation?

The active flagellant wants to punish. The passive partner wants to be punished. Of course both need a reason for these wishes. As jealousy plays an all-overshadowing part in lesbianism and as lesbians do not have the reputation of being very faithful to each other, both partners most of the time have a reason for flagellation. The active one because she is jealous. The passive one because she was unfaithful and now wants to be punished.

Sometimes jealousy in lesbians can express itself in a very strange way.

167

Wilhelm Stekel in his book on masturbation and homo-sexuality[2] mentions a very interesting case-history. The patient was the forty-five-year-old wife of a doctor who told Stekel:

"I need your help as I live in a situation that embitters my whole life and that turns my marriage into a real hell. I've been married now for twenty-two years and I can easily say there hasn't been one single happy day in my life up till now, except when my husband was alone with me and didn't have the opportunity of seeing another woman. He is a doctor and when we were engaged to be married I was already jealous of his patients. Before that time I'd never been jealous. If I had been, I wouldn't have married my husband. When we were engaged I was only jealous of my women friends and of acquaintances, particularly if they were very beautiful. After our marriage the situation got worse and worse. During his consulting-hours I waited behind the door and had goose-flesh from excitement. My man is a gynaecologist and a very famous one at that! I asked him many times to give up this profession and to choose another speciality. Strange as it seems, before we married the fact that he was a gynaecologist had excited me very much and had settled the matter when I decided to marry him. I thought then: this man sees so many beautiful women when they are naked and yet he has chosen me! That thought flattered me very much. But this was only in the beginning. Very soon I became very jealous.

"I had a very beautiful friend who was getting treatment from my husband. I can't tell you what I've gone through while she was with him. I imagined: now she's getting out of her blouse and now she's getting out of her petticoat. Now he is looking at her breasts. Now she's seating herself in the chair . . . now she is spreading her legs . . . I felt the tortures of hell. I was sure my husband wouldn't be able to resist this woman and I was quite sure he would kiss her. I quarrelled with him and I quarrelled with my friend who broke with me.

"During our marriage all this was getting worse and worse. I tormented my husband so much that he permitted me to watch the goings-on in his consulting-room by means of a peep-hole. Now I could prove to myself that my husband was faithful to me. It was no use. At that moment I was already convinced of the fact that he was sexually stimulated by the presence of his naked patients but didn't want to show it or to admit it to me! From now on I repeated it daily: give up your profession!

"Years passed and we never stopped quarrelling. My daughter grew up and married and I thought my jealousy would disappear as I grew older. But it didn't disappear! It is getting worse and worse. Now I'm already jealous of my son-in-law, on my daughter's account! Fortunately she has no reason to be jealous and she just laughs at me . . .

"I think I'm also jealous of my daughter. I'd like to have her love all for my own and I grudge her her husband. She married a rich man of noble character, but I wasn't satisfied and treated my son-in-law like dirt. I was sick of my own conduct, but I really couldn't help it. I have consulted already the most famous psychiatrists. Professor X gave me a hypnotic treatment. I left my husband and stayed on my own for three long months. All in vain."

Stekel comments on this interesting case-history:

"What was the meaning of this jealousy? The cause of it was an unconscious homosexuality. She was jealous of her friend because she herself loves her. She identifies herself with the part of the gynaecologist, her husband, and admits to herself that in that case she wouldn't be able to resist the temptation. She identifies herself so wrongly with the part of the male in this situation that she herself feels stimulated by looking at these women patients. The peep-hole isn't only useful because it appeases her jealousy, but also because it gives her the opportunity to play the part of a voyeur. In this way she could feast her eyes on the goings-on in the consulting-room! This daily guard at the peep-hole is her homosexual stimulation, that enflames her. It is her husband whom she wants to extinguish her passions.

"After I had explained all this to her an important improvement set in. This woman realised also she felt a homosexual love for her daughter. It was this love that inspired her jealousy of her son-in-law."

JEALOUS OF HER MAID . . .

Unexpected as the cause of this woman's jealousy was, the situation—her man being a gynaecologist etc.—is still more or less understandable. However, sometimes daily occurrences that have a seemingly obvious cause, prove once again that appearances are deceptive. Another case-history mentioned by Stekel[3] is that of a thirty-year-old, newly-married woman who also was tormented by jealousy:

"She engaged a parlour-maid who was very young and a little bit coquettish, but whom she liked at first sight. A week later she was already jealous and felt that her husband, who never took notice of maids before, gave this girl too much attention and behaved in far too friendly a way towards her. She imagined he even looked provokingly at her. At first she kept silent as she was ashamed to talk it over with her husband. But then she told him he had to behave more severely towards the girl.

"Her husband laughed at her and told her he behaved towards this maid in the same way he did towards the others. He told her she imagined things. This maid worked well and there was no reason to be severe. These words gave her for a very short while some reassurance. She didn't lose sight of her husband for a single moment and soon concluded he liked the girl very much. At night she woke up several times and then went to the maid's room to check on her. One night her husband didn't feel well and had to leave his bed a few times. She was convinced this was only a pretext to go to the girl. She worried about it and left her bed to walk up and down the ice-cold corridor outside the bedroom. Her husband asked what was

170

the matter with her and she told him she was worried because of his illness.

"At last her jealousy came out into the open and she reproached him with his attitude towards the maid and told him she was convinced she was his mistress. Her husband was furious and asked her to dismiss the girl at once. Only then, he told her, would the house be quiet again. To his surprise she told him she wouldn't dream of dismissing the maid. She was a girl who worked well and had a wonderful personality. It would be very difficult, she told him, to find a nice girl like her for the second time. She again asked her husband to act more severely towards the girl and made him swear on oath that she wasn't his mistress.

"Towards the girl she felt a strange fury she couldn't explain. She thought of throwing herself at the girl and hitting her. She didn't understand these thoughts as she had never hit a maid. Nevertheless she was stimulated by the thought of being able to hit this girl who gave her so much misery already. She had to check herself so as not to lose her self-control. While talking to the girl she was very easily irritated and peremptory.

"Notwithstanding these difficulties she couldn't force herself to dismiss the maid. At the same time she felt scared when she had to be alone with the girl.

"All these phenomena were caused by homosexual feelings with regard to the girl, who was a very striking blonde indeed. She herself loved the girl and therefore couldn't understand that her husband didn't desire her. Her way of thinking was: if I was a man, I would make this girl my mistress at once. A very interesting phenomenon was the fury she felt and the desire to hit the girl. Her love is transformed into the contrary, and her desire to touch the girl (to feel her body against her own!) is transformed into a desire to hit her. How many contacts, that originated in rage and take the shape of blows, punches, etc., are born out of love that is transformed into hate!

"I made it clear to this woman that she had to dismiss

171

the maid. Now she understood the cause of her jealousy. After the dismissal of the girl all the phenomena described disappeared."

Now we have made it clear that jealousy plays a very important role in female homosexuality, it is much easier to understand the appearance of sado-masochistic tendencies in lesbian relationships.

THE GIRL WHO HATED HER LOVER...

Up till now the cases we mentioned had as a subject women whose homosexuality was suppressed or unconscious. In cases in which the subject is a straight homosexual, jealousy also plays as important a part.

A striking example of sado-masochistic behaviour in a lesbian relationship is the case of Gertrud D. She was a thirty-one-year-old artist and had had for several years a homosexual relationship with a girl of twenty-six, called Gaby, who worked as a reporter for a newspaper. The reason Gertrud wanted to consult me was her growing sadistic attitude towards Gaby—an attitude that alarmed her, as she was afraid that she would kill the girl one day. She had read the story of Alice Mitchell and Freda Ward[4], two lesbians who made headlines in American newspapers in 1892 when nineteen-year-old Alice killed her seventeen-year-old friend. Alice later committed suicide.

"It was a sadistic murder," Gertrud said. "Maybe you know Alice slashed Freda's throat with a razor." She looked at me silently for a few moments and then said very softly: "Doctor . . . I'm scared. I'm scared to death, because I'm sure that some day poor Gaby . . ." She could not finished her sentence, shook her head and whispered: "And yet I love her. I love her so much. That scares me too . . . Before Alice Mitchell killed her friend she wrote her: 'You are my own sweet love—the darling of my life. I know you are true to me, love, and I more than idolise

172

you.' I could have written these words to Gaby. I love her so much and yet I'm sure one day she'll die by my hand . . ."

It was clear to me Gertrude was at her wits' end. I began with reassuring her.

"If you've read something about the killing of Freda Ward, you know Alice Mitchell thought she had a reason to kill her friend," I said. "Besides, this was in 1892 in Memphis, Tennessee, then one of the most backward parts of the United States! I don't think it's right to compare Alice's situation with yours! "

"Alice Mitchell killed her loved one," she said. "That is the thing that counts. Not where or when it has happened."

"No, Gertrud," I said quietly. "You're wrong. There is something else that counts. I mentioned it to you already. Alice Mitchell thought she had a reason to kill Freda Ward. She did it out of despair. If you've read about her, you know that. Long before she killed Freda, Alice tried to commit suicide because of her friend's interest in a young man. Then Freda saw the error of her ways and during a reconciliation scene, Alice gratefully gave her a diamond ring and asked Freda to marry her. Alice promised to have her hair cut short and to wear men's clothes. Before this marriage was contracted, Alice's family stepped in and all the plans were frustrated. Then and only then Alice killed her homosexual 'bride'. She slashed Freda's throat because, as she later stated, she loved her so much that she couldn't live without her. I don't think this was true, for when she killed Freda, she knew she had to live without her from that moment on! The reason Alice killed her lover was, I think, a cool reasoning: if I cannot have her—nobody will have her. It was a horrible deed arising from despair and I don't think you're right when you compare your situation with the situation Alice and Freda lived in."

Gertrud had listened without saying a word. When I was silent she slowly nodded.

173

"Maybe you're right, doctor. To tell the truth I never thought of that. Nevertheless I'm still afraid our love-making will become so violent that one day I will kill Gaby involuntarily."

Now she did not think any longer of Alice Mitchell and did not compare herself any longer with that unfortunate girl, it was easier to talk with her about the things that disturbed her.

"You know, doctor," she said pensively. "Though Gaby and I have known each other now for a number of years, we are still very much in love with each other . . . And yet there is this strange hatred I sometimes experience when making love to her. Suddenly she abhors me . . . I want to hurt her and consequently I hit her and bite her . . . She never resists . . . I think she doesn't mind . . . As a matter of fact, I suspect she likes it as it seems to give her more sexual gratification. But you should see her when it is over! She has bruises all over her body and there have been times she wasn't able to sit down for two or three days . . ." She shook her head. "Don't think I enjoy hurting her . . . I mean . . . when it is over I feel terribly sorry. Sometimes I cry over what I have done and then she has to comfort me. She always forgives me for what I've done and I . . . Of course I promise not to do it again, but a few weeks later I hit her again . . . It always happens when I suddenly discover I hate and abhor her . . . Yet at the same moment I know how much I love Gaby . . . I don't know what's the matter with me . . . Please, doctor, help me . . ."

"When you treat Gaby cruelly, do you get any sexual stimulation out of it?"

She thought very seriously before she answered. Then she shrugged and said reflectingly:

"I . . . I don't know . . . Of course when this happens there seems to be more sexual excitement in it for both of us than at other times. But I really can't say I enjoy being cruel to her."

174

"You say you love Gaby very much. Are you sure she loves you too?"

"Of course I'm sure!" She really took that question badly. "If she didn't love me, do you think she would have stayed with me all these years? After all I have made her go through? Of course she loves me. And I love her!"

"I'm sorry I upset you, Gertrud," I said quietly. "But please understand I have to ask these questions if I want to help you."

"Go on," she grumbled.

"Now I have to ask you another rather intimate question, and I really do hope you will not take it badly, for . . ."

"Stop beating around the bush. What's the question?"

"All right. Are you a faithful lover?"

She smiled suddenly.

"That's what I call an intimate question. All right. The answer is yes. Yes, I'm a very faithful lover. If there is someone I love—I mean really love—I'm not going to deceive her by hopping into bed with others."

I knew she spoke the truth. In her way Gertrud was strictly a one-woman girl.

"Good. Now tell me about Gaby. Would you say she is as faithful to you as you are to her?"

She thought for a few moments, then shook her head and said:

"No. I'm afraid I can't say she is." She smiled apologetically. "Don't get me wrong, doctor. Gaby is a wonderful girl and I love her very much. But in this regard she is just . . . well, different. I think you could say our characters are different. She can't help it, I mean . . . If she had the same character as I have, maybe she would be faithful to me, but I . . . well, maybe I wouldn't love her."

During the sessions I had with Gertrud it appeared that her attitude towards her friend was close to a love-hate relationship. There were moments she felt she was through with Gaby and that she hated her and despised her. The next moment she felt she loved the girl as she had loved nobody else. These emotions made it clear Gertrud had a very unstable personality and she found it very difficult to keep it under control.

I learned some interesting details about her childhood and got the impression that at no time in her life had she been in a position in which she had to keep a check on herself and her emotions. Being an artist she was as free as she wished and only very seldom met with a situation that restricted her liberty. Gertrud definitely had very strong sado-masochistic components in her personality. The masochist in her enjoyed the fact that Gaby was untrue to her. About once a month the sadist in her awoke and made her punish her friend for her unfaithfulness. As she enjoyed being cruel to Gaby and Gaby clearly liked being punished both of them experienced greater sexual excitement out of these punishments than normal love-play could give.

It was the memory of Gaby's unfaithfulness that worked as a trigger on Gertrud's latent sadism. To camouflage this sadistic behaviour for a great part, she felt a strange hatred towards Gaby—a hatred she could not explain but that was for some part also a consequence of her instability.

I explained to Gertrud she need not be afraid that one day, as she stated it, she "would kill Gaby involuntarily". Gaby was a strong, rather heavily built girl and being no fool she surely would stop the "loving punishment" if it reached the point where she could not get enjoyment out of it any more.

"But what shall I do now?" Gertrud asked.

"If I were you, I wouldn't do a thing," I said. "The point is both of you like your relationship as it is now. You were right when you told me Gaby would have left you a long time ago if she hadn't loved you. The only one who has some objection is you yourself, Gertrud. You didn't understand your own actions and that disturbed you. Now you know more about the cause and background, I shouldn't worry about it any more if I were you! Just try

176

to get a better check on yourself. You might be able then
to improve your personality. Don't worry about Gaby. I'm
quite sure she's perfectly happy."

A LESBIAN SEX MURDER

A striking example of sadism in lesbians was the grue-
some murder that was committed in 1897 in a brothel in
the Austrian city of Graz and since has been described by
psychiatrists as a typical lesbian sex murder. Kratter[5] gives
the following description:

"On the night of May 16 or May 17 of the year 1897 a
most horrible event occurred in a brothel in Graz. M.O., a
girl who worked in the house as a parlour- and kitchen-
maid, was stabbed to death with a long kitchen knife by
the woman who owned the brothel. The injuries of heart,
lungs and liver that caused the girl's death will not be discussed here. It was the motive of the murder that was
unique.

"It soon appeared that the woman who committed the
murder had had sexual relations with her victim. She was
in the habit of locking in herself and the girl for hours on
end and very often the girl spent a whole night in bed with
her mistress. All the inmates of the house knew of this
relationship. M.O. worked not as a prostitute but as maid
in the house and sexual intercourse with men was something she was not allowed to have. She was only permitted
to make love with her mistress.

"On the day she died, M.O. returned from an eight-day
visit to her relatives. The brothel-owner received her in a
very excited mood. During O.'s absence she had been
very irritated and had shown strong feelings of jealousy.
She worried because she thought O. would use the opportunity of being away to have sexual intercourse with men.
Soon after O.'s return the woman locked herself and the
girl in her bedroom. After about an hour and a half the

177

inmates of the house heard a shout and after that some noise and a piercing cry for help. They ran to the bedroom and assembled in front of the still-locked door. They tried to open it, but in vain. Suddenly the door was unlocked on the inside and a blood-covered O., clothed only in a chemise, rushed out of the room. She was pursued by a wildly gesticulating brothel-owner who stabbed the girl with a long kitchen knife. O. fled to the garden. There her mistress overtook her and gave her some more stabs till the girl fell down and died. It all happened very quickly and the frightened girls did not have the time to overpower the furious woman.

"There was one remarkable injury that made this case unique. The nose of the girl was entirely bitten off. This must have happened when both women were still in bed or when O. prepared to leave the room. Anyhow it must have caused O.'s first cry. The bitten-off nose was soon found in a corner of the room. Policemen who found it concluded that the woman must have spat it there.

"Those who know the psychological relation between lust and cruelty know there is more to this than only a case of a very rare injury of the nose. Here we meet lust that at its height turned into cruelty. The passionate kiss turns into the wild bite of a madwoman. The lust to love turns into lust to kill. The heterosexual nymphomaniac gives herself to any man and consequently must be a masochist. The homosexual passionate woman must be a sadist, who treats women in the same cruel way male sadists do. Her victim can only be a woman."

Stekel, who comments on Kratter's theory, wonders if Kratter is right. He states that many lesbians have masochistic tendencies with regard to women, but almost always sadistic ones with regard to men. To illustrate his point he cites a newspaper-report. It is an item about two lesbians who—both being married—decided to poison their husbands. One of them, the thirty-two-year-old Emma Klein, succeeded in killing her husband by administering

178

quantities of arsenic to his food. When her mother-in-law became suspicious the body was exhumed. Soon after she was arrested, Emma Klein confessed. Her friend was arrested and both women were sent to prison.

Stekel not only mentions this case to prove his theory that masochistic lesbians can be sadistic in their relations with men, but also to confirm his statement that among homosexuals the rate of criminality is higher than among heterosexuals. All the same, to confirm an important statement like this, one needs of course more facts than this one newspaper item! The statistical material available up till now (for instance, Kinsey) makes it more probable, however, that the percentage of criminals among homosexuals is about the same as the percentage among heterosexuals.

More safely can it be said that most homosexuals—male homosexuals in particular—have some striking qualities in common, though I do not follow Bergler[6] who speaks of a "special mental attitude of homosexuals". Nevertheless, it is a curious fact that a great many male homosexuals succeed in keeping a boyish, often even childish appearance till they are forty or fifty years old—or even older. Havelock Ellis, who commented on this phenomenon, thought it had something to do with the infantile personality of many homosexuals. It is this infantility that causes the hatred of "growing up" every homosexual cherishes. Havelock Ellis observed many homosexuals choose green as their favourite colour: "a colour best loved by children and very young girls". He noticed that most homosexuals were talented actors. Their vanity and their almost feminine love for ornaments and jewellery also pointed to a personality that had not completely matured and was still for a part infantile. All these characteristics refer chiefly to male homosexuals. However, the personality of the female homosexual is also not developed completely. Her infantile characteristics are the origin of her often masculine interests and appearance. Homosexuality—be it male or female—is childhood's bisexuality gone wrong.

179

Childhood is still clearly visible in the often infantile personality of the male or female homosexual. The bisexuality and the extent to which it went wrong can be seen in his or her behaviour in relation to the members of the same sex.

NOTES

1. The word was invented by the American author Philip Wylie who wrote a number of books with critical views of life in the American society.

2. Wilhelm Stekel: *Onanie und Homosexualität*, Berlin 1923.

3. Ibid.

4. More details about this murder can be found in the article "Lesbian Love Murder" by O. D. Cauldwell in *Sexology Magazine* for July 1950.

5. Kratter: *Gerichtsärtzliche Praxis*, Berlin 1919.

6. Edmund Bergler: *Homosexuality, Disease or Way of Life?*, New York 1956.

CHAPTER TWELVE

Once a Lesbian—Always a Lesbian?

As mentioned already in our historical survey, it would be wrong to think that lesbianism is something that can be found only in parts of the world we call civilised. The fact that it did play an important role in ancient Greece, that it reigned supreme during the eighteenth century and has celebrated its comeback in our modern Western world does not mean, as we have in fact already shown, that female homosexuality is not to be found in less developed communities around the world.

Among African tribes lesbianism is a well known phenomenon. The Ovaherero, a tribe of the Bantus, call lesbians Omapanga. Parents know and approve of the lesbian relationships of their daughters. Sometimes parents bring about contacts between a homosexual daughter and other lesbians, in the same way they look for a husband for their heterosexual daughters.

On the island of Zanzibar lesbians sometimes have relations with heterosexual women who get paid for their services. According to Baumann[1] female homosexuals at Zanzibar have three ways of getting sexual satisfaction: licking (kulambana), rubbing the sexual parts against the sexual parts of the partner (kusagana) and a pseudocoition by way of an artificial penis principally made of ivory (kujitia mbo ya mpingo).

The artificial penis has considerable size and is manufactured by artisans. Sometimes these instruments take the

181

shape of a double penis and can be used at both ends by two women at the same time. Most times a narrow canal is bored through the artificial penis. When the instrument is used it is filled with warm water. When orgasm is reached, the water is squeezed out and ejaculation is imitated. According to the island's population the artificial penis is an invention of the Arabs and is used particularly in Arabian harems.

In South Africa among the Bantus lesbian relationships in which love plays an important part are not well known, although mutual masturbation amongst these women is commonplace. It is practised in public and a very popular pastime.

Mutual masturbation is a beloved theme of folk tales. One wonders if the extraordinary size of the clitoris that can be found with the Bantu women is not the consequence of their exaggerated practice of masturbation . . . a phenomenon as we have seen with the Bush- and Hottentot-women too.

The North American Indians knew female homosexuality before they met the first white man. According to legend the population of New Caledonia became reduced because more and more women refused to have sexual relations with men and learned to give sexual satisfaction to each other. Karsch-Haack[2] gives interesting information about female homosexuality among South American Indians:

"Among the Tupi-tribe in Brazil women can be found who made a vow never to have sexual relations with men. They take this vow very seriously and would give their life to keep it. These individuals never give in to the daily pursuits of their sex. They imitate men in all details and give the appearance that they have stopped being women. They wear their hair cut short and accompany the men when they go to war or if there is a hunt. They are

182

very skilled with bow and arrow and are feared by the enemies of the tribe. Every one of these women has a young girl who acts as her servant and whom she considers to be her wife. They live together as if in matrimony."

Among the tribes of north-east Asia lesbianism is well known. In Kamtschatka women have sexual relations with women by way of the clitoris, which they call the *bolschaia reka netschitsch*. Before making love with another woman, these women first have passionate sexual relations with dogs.

This enumeration will make it clear again that lesbianism is not a disease of our civilisation. On the contrary, it seems to be one of the many fairly normal outlets of human energy. All over the world, even in the darkest jungle, female homosexuals can be found. Of course it is relatively easy to look for causes of homosexuality in civilised men and women and to come up with a number of elements that can shape a homosexual personality. As the true origin of homosexuality is still not exposed, every acceptable theory is a step forward. One must take care, however, not to consider homosexuality too much as a phenomenon of our civilisation.

We know nothing of the workings of the mind of a savage. We only know that his unconsciousness plays a more important part in the make-up of his personality than his consciousness. Jung observed that uncivilised man lives mainly from out of the "universal unconsciousness" and has therefore a very undeveloped personality. With this in mind it is rather risky to put down homosexuality to causes to be found in modern, civilised family life. For in that case what is the origin of homosexuality among uncivilised people? If we say a girl becomes a lesbian because of an insufficient rapport between her and her mother and an exaggerated rapport between her and the father, how can a girl in the Brazilian jungle become a homosexual, as she is exclusively brought up by her mother and never meets her father?

Homosexuality still is a mystery. About the causes we can at most guess and an infallible cure still is not to be found. I think a man like Edmund Bergler gives false hope to thousands of male and female homosexuals when he writes that every homosexual can be "cured" if only he or she wants to. I have seen too many men and women who tried and tried and could not be rid of their homosexuality. Of course in very many cases a homosexual can be "cured", but a close analysis in such a case results in the conclusion that the individual who received treatment was never exclusively homosexual. The best result one can get in treating a straight homosexual is to change the patient into a man or woman with bisexual interests. I still have to meet the first man or woman who by means of treatment changed his or her interests from exclusively homosexual into exclusively heterosexual.

Maybe this sounds rather gloomy to homosexuals who want to be "normal" people, but I think it is better to tell the truth than to raise hopes in vain.

A sure sign that there still is not found an infallible cure for homosexuality is the fact that almost every year new "infallible" cures are found. One of the latest treatments was invented by American psychiatrists and found its origin in Pavlov's theory of the conditioned reflex. Lesbians who want to make use of this treatment are shown into a dark room. Soft music is heard and pictures of handsome naked men are projected on a screen. Then very unpleasant noises are heard and on the screen appear pictures of females. Every picture of women that is projected is accompanied by a palpable and extremely unpleasant electric shock that is administered to the patient. The inventors of the treatment claim they were able to cure many homosexuals this way. I have my doubts about these cures.

Margrit came to me because she wanted to be cured of her homosexuality. She was a fashion photographer and thirty-six years old. The reason she wanted to be a heterosexual was that she felt very lonely and wanted to marry and have children, a very positive desire that—alas!—is not sufficient to guarantee a positive result. I decided to use psychoanalysis as this was the treatment that gave the best chance of succeeding. Bravely Margrit started a long row of sessions.

She was a very sympathetic girl with a handsome, suntanned face that gave her the appearance of an outdoor girl. For three years she came to me, driven by an ardent desire to find happiness as a normal, heterosexual girl. Then I broke off the treatment and told her that is was only a waste of time and money to go on.

During countless sessions I had heard everything about her, her work, her childhood, her dreams and her relations. I had succeeded in rousing in her a more lively interest in men, but I had not been able to take away that dark urge that drove her to members of her own sex.

"You know, doctor," she said once. "Now I know why I'm a lesbian. It is all very clear. I know why I want to find sexual satisfaction at the hands of women. I understand that my childhood experiences gave me an aversion to men and I know that I can conquer that aversion. And yet there is still one thing I do not understand . . ." She looked puzzled.

"What is it, Margrit?" I asked.

"You have made all these things clear and I know now more about myself than I ever did and yet . . . there is one thing that I don't understand. Why, doctor . . . why does my heart start beating restlessly when I see a beautiful girl in the street? Why do I fall in love with her—though I don't want to? Why do I want to touch her . . . to kiss her . . . to love her and make her mine?"

185

At the end of her psychoanalysis I knew I'd never succeed in wiping out all traces of lesbianism. Margrit was an example of my thesis that all one can do for a homosexual is to try to change him or her into a bisexual. I know that to most psychiatrists bisexuality does not exist inherently, but it is a way of defining a person who can be sexually interested in members of both sexes.

"This is really all I can do for you, Margrit," I said during our last session. "You're able to feel interest now for men too, and that will give you a better chance of marrying and having children, but I cannot guarantee that never more in your life will you feel love for members of your own sex. We have both tried to give you a new personality and I think we succeeded up to a certain point. Beyond that point we cannot go."

"That means I still have homosexual tendencies?"

"Yes. But don't forget almost every human being has them. The perfectly male man and the perfectly female woman may exist in novels and on the screen; in everyday life you won't be able to find them. I think most of us are unconscious of our homosexual feelings and this can harm the personality to a great extent. You at least have the advantage of being conscious of it . . ."

She nodded.

"You mean I'll have to learn to live with it when I'm married?"

"Yes, but it isn't as tragic as you think. Most people have learned to live with their sexual peculiarities. There are married male homosexuals, exhibitionists, fetishists, masochists and sadists who have adapted themselves to married life and are wonderful family men now. Why shouldn't a woman with homosexual tendencies be a good mother and housewife? As long as you know this urge exists in you it cannot leap out of the shadows of your personality unexpectedly. Be honest with your future husband. Tell him who and what you are and try to make him

186

understand you. Then, I think, your marriage will be a success."

Margrit eventually married. Her husband owns a small advertising agency. They are very happy together. Two years ago a son was born and once she brought him with her to visit me.

"I'm very grateful to you, doctor," she said. "You changed me into another woman. Yes, you did! I'm very glad you didn't put my expectations too high . . . You didn't promise to cure me completely, because you thought you wouldn't be able to do that."

"Tell me, Margrit," I said. "How's the lesbian inside you?"

She smiled.

"I haven't been hearing from her for a few months," she said. "About half a year ago I met Victor's new secretary, a nice dark girl of nineteen and suddenly that old 'butch' inside of me reared her head. But it was only a caprice . . . I think I'm too busy now to spend a lot of time looking at beautiful girls. I've my husband and my son and I'm happy—thanks to you, doctor."

"What about the future, Margrit?"

Again she smiled.

" 'Butch' and I will grow old gracefully," she said. "I'll always know she's there, right inside of me, and she'll always know I keep an eye on her. In that way we both have to watch our steps!"

I was glad that was the way Margrit thought about it. In my lifetime I had seen too many unhappy and lonesome lesbians not to hope that at least some of them would find the strength and the energy to change their lives.

Many very sensational books about lesbianism have been published lately. Some authors, not hindered by the least amount of knowledge of the subject, have helped only to enlarge the misconception the public has of lesbianism as a whole. Too many men and women still consider homosexuals—be they male or female—as "creeps" and ask for laws that "stamp out the perversion of homosexuality". Others think homosexuals are people that can be "converted". Alas, it is not all that easy.

Not only among ordinary men and women is there still a great misunderstanding of "the facts of life". Many, many authorities—judges, policemen, politicians—do not know the basic things about a phenomenon like homosexuality, that is coming more and more into the open every day. Yet these authorities foster public opinion and decide the view society takes with regard to the countless men and women who are for reasons outside their control homosexuals and now try to make the best of their life. I think this is a frightening fact.

If we want to have a better world, we have to strive for a better understanding of our fellow men. That means we will also have to accept the existence of ideas and habits we think strange or even repulsive. To be able to accept them, we first have to understand them. To help those who are sincerely interested in understanding the lesbian and lesbianism, this book has been written.

NOTES

1. Oskar Baumann: "Conträre Sexual-Erscheinungen bei der Neger-Bevölkerung Zanzibars". *Zeitschrift für Ethnologie*. Vol. 6, Berlin 1899.

2. F. Karsch-Haack: "Uranismus oder Päderastie und Tribadie bei den Naturvölkern" in *Jahrbuch für Sexuelle Zwischenstufen*, vol. 3. Leipzig 1902. On the subject of male homosexuality Karsch-Haack gives interesting information particularly about homosexuality among tribes that up till then had been considered as being "unspoiled by the of civilised western man".

INDEX

191